Getting What You Want

Success can be yours if you follow the *Power Play* techniques revealed in this book. The author has made them work for him, and by following his dynamic plan you too can make it to the top.

Getting What You Want

You Want

POWER PLAY TECHNIQUES FOR ACHIEVING SUCCESS

by

J.H. Brennan

THORSONS PUBLISHERS LIMITED
Wellingborough, Northamptonshire

This edition published 1985

British Library Cataloguing in Publication Data

Brennan, J. H.
  Getting what you want.
  1. Success
  I. Title
  158'.1   BF637.S8

  ISBN 0-7225-1177-9

Printed in Great Britain by
Richard Clay (The Chaucer Press) Ltd,
Bungay, Suffolk

Contents

DEDICATION

For Paddy Geogeghan, one of Ireland's finest salesmen, who helped me formulate the principals of Power Play; for his lovely wife Una, one of the most efficient executives I have ever known; and for my dear friend Anne L. Brennan, founder and director of the Dublin Relaxation Centre, at whose clinic many clients have benefitted from the techniques advocated in the initial section of this book. Thanks to you all. I owe you more than I could ever say.

ACKNOWLEDGEMENT

In preparing the Self Image Quiz which makes up most of Chapter Two, I received enormous assistance from an American doctor who generously devoted time to formulating several of the questions and constructively criticizing my initial draft of the remainder. Medical ethics do not permit me to name him, but I would like publicly to acknowledge my debt to him with sincere gratitude.

PART ONE

Introducing Power Play

This section deals with general success techniques relating to your public and your private life. In Part Two success is related much more closely to the business situation.

But it's vital you grasp the principles covered in these early chapters. Because they form the foundation on which you'll build an interesting, worthwhile and prosperous career.

1

The Vital Key

Thirteen years ago, I stumbled on a secret so revolutionary that it changed my life. It's a secret I plan to share with you. Right here and now, on the very first page of this book. Although the implications are far-reaching, the secret itself can be expressed in just four words:

YOUR LIMITATIONS ARE IMAGINARY.

I don't expect you to believe this—yet. I don't expect you to take my word for it, even though those four words make up the most important single statement in this book. But if I can convince you that that statement is true, then I've given you a vital key. A key that will unlock a vast potential you never even knew you had. A key that will, quite literally, change your life as it changed mine.

What does it mean, that statement on your limitations? When most people say a thing's imaginary, they mean it's unreal, it doesn't exist. Am I trying to tell you your limitations don't exist? That you don't have any limitations at all? That there's absolutely nothing in the world you can't do? Hardly. We both know some things that are plain impossible. Try touching your right elbow with your right hand, for instance. Or stopping the tide like King Canute.

But there's one thing about genuine impossibilities. They're never all that important. Who *needs* to stop the tide?

You can live a full and happy life without *ever* touching your right elbow with your right hand. And leaving aside impossibilities, that statement about your limitations means there is nothing—absolutely nothing—you cannot achieve. This is so important, I want to spell it out. I want to make sure there's absolutely no chance of misunderstanding between us.

If you want to make a million pounds—you can. If you want to make *ten* million pounds—you can. If you want to be popular—you can. If you want prestige, or a better job, or a bigger house, or a faster car, or a jet plane, or gold taps on your bath, or fame, or adventure . . . you can have them all. Once you come to accept the truth embodied in those four little words: *your limitations are imaginary*.

Of course, it's easy to tell you a secret like that, but only a fool would take it at face value. After all, you *know* you have limitations that have nothing to do with impossibilities. You know, for instance, that you'll never make a million (even though you also know making a million's not impossible: Paul Getty made several—and he's not the only one). You *know* you will never be famous, or achieve even a fraction of your childhood ambitions. This is *facing up to reality*, isn't it? Year in and year out, people all over the country are taught that this is the sensible way to think; even the sane way to think. Which is one reason why success comes to the very few.

Here's Proof
Let's get down to business. Until I *prove* to you your limitations are imaginary, you're naturally going to keep right on in that old 'sane and sensible' way of thinking. And as long as you keep right on in that old 'sane and sensible' way of thinking, your chances of personal success are exactly zero.

We'll start with a very simple example. Suppose I arrived at your house carrying a plank. The plank is twenty-one feet long, one-and-a-half feet wide and six inches thick. Suppose I laid this on the ground outside your house and offered you £100 to walk the full length of the plank—twenty-one feet from end to end. Do you think, for £100, you could manage this simple task?

Of course you could! There's not a doubt in your head. You'd skip along that plank like a three-year-old, and in about seven seconds flat you'd be counting your money and wondering what sort of nut I was to make you an offer like that.

But suppose instead of laying the plank along the ground, I laid it instead between two cliffs. So that now, instead of lying on the ground, the plank forms a narrow bridge across a twenty-foot wide chasm. And that chasm's deep, nearly half a mile of a drop straight down onto jagged rocks with a river full of piranha fish boiling between them. Would you still walk across that plank for £100? Or £200? Or £500? You probably wouldn't even listen to my offer, no matter how high I went. Because walking across a one-and-a-half foot wide bridge over a chasm is likely to cost you your life. You'd look down at that sheer drop onto those jagged rocks and that boiling river and you'd know, as sure as sunrise, that you'd never make it even half way over.

But when you stop to think about it, the distance you have to walk hasn't changed. And the plank hasn't changed. And your ability to walk hasn't changed. So why is it that in one case you can walk the plank easily and collect your £100, while in another you simply couldn't walk the plank at all, even for five times that amount?

The answer is imagination. That's the one factor that has really changed between the two situations. In the first, you had no difficulty at all imagining yourself walking along the plank. In the second, all you could imagine was falling off it, plunging down into the abyss and smashing on the jagged rocks below. In the first case, you did not stop to imagine you had any limitations, so you walked the plank with ease. In the second case, you imagined all sorts of limitations and the result was that you could not walk the plank at all. Worse still, if you had somehow *forced* yourself to walk out on the plank across that chasm, your imagination would have made sure you *did* fall off. So your imaginary limitations are real enough all right. But that doesn't make them any less imaginary.

A Personal Example

Let's take another, more realistic example. This one is from personal experience—a case that actually happened.

Seven or eight years ago, my secretary introduced me to her fiancé, a personable young man I'll now call John. I was very taken with John. He dressed well, looked good and had more than his fair share of charm. But he was in an utterly dead-end job. He drove a van and delivered tinned goods to grocers. John wasn't happy in his job. He knew its limitations. He knew he had no chance of promotion. He knew the experience he was getting wouldn't fit him for a better job elsewhere. Most serious of all, the job paid so little that he wasn't able to save any money; and until he could save some money, he couldn't get married to my secretary, which was the one thing in the world he most wanted to do.

When John told me all this, it struck me instantly that he was wasting his time as a van delivery man. He had exactly the sort of looks and personality which go to make up a first-class salesman. And as luck would have it, I'd noticed in the morning paper an advertisement seeking salesmen for a company which manufactured shampoo and other hair-care products. I suggested to him that he should apply.

But John would have none of it. He was 'realistic' and 'recognized his limitations'. He had come from a working class background and his education finished when he left primary school. He had no experience of selling and 'knew' he would be useless at it. And the only thing he knew about hair was that you should wash it when it gets dirty. With all these limitations, it was obvious to John that he would never land a sales job with a shampoo company, so it was pointless even making an application. I tried to convince him that education was far less important than personality in selling. I pointed out that the ad did not specify that selling experience was essential, but mentioned training would be given. It was useless. John maintained that with his background he wouldn't even get as far as the initial interview.

Eventually I made a deal with him. I *guaranteed* I would get him as far as the initial interview if he was prepared to go along and try his best to make a good impression. John agreed . . . reluctantly. He may have thought I had some inside contacts with the firm in question to enable me to guarantee an interview. I hadn't. I simply knew that when a company goes to the trouble and expense of advertising for untrained staff, they will interview *any* applicant whose letter of application doesn't mark him out as a moron. I made sure John's initial letter was up to standard. I wrote it myself and had him sign it.

John got the interview and the job. But left alone, he would have done neither. And what would have stopped him was not his lack of education, experience or know-how. What would have stopped him was *imaginary limitations*, limitations which existed only in his head and did not correspond to outside reality.

The Power of Imagination
Very few people realize the enormous power vested in the imagination, and those who do tend to keep the secret to themselves. Over the past few years, the martial arts of the Orient—judo, karate, kung-fu and the rest—have become increasingly popular in the West. But Oriental teachers, happy to demonstrate holds, throws, kicks and nerve-points, almost always hold back a vital aspect of these arts—their *mental* disciplines. And central to these disciplines is the use of the imagination. When, for example, a kung-fu master is locked in a particularly difficult hold, he is trained to *imagine* himself breaking free. Before he makes any move to break the hold, before he applies a single ounce of pressure, before he engages in the slightest struggle, his teachers have instructed him to *visualize himself succeeding*. Furthermore, Orientals well versed in these arts maintain that unless a fighter can see himself breaking free, he will never break free. That's the degree of importance they place on the use of imagination.

Although the Orient is generally far behind the West in the application of purely physical techniques, it is centuries ahead in the realms of psychology. And psychology's important, because the first step on the road to personal success is taken right inside your head. Success isn't luck, or hard work, or good judgements—although these factors undoubtedly play a part in some success stories. Success, more than anything else, is an attitude of mind, and that attitude begins with the realization that *your limitations are imaginary*.

You may feel by now I'm overstressing this point. I'm not. That single realization is so important to your personal success that everything else in this book is secondary to it. In fact, once you've been absolutely and totally convinced about the truth of those four words, you could stop reading at once and still achieve the success you desire. It might be just a little harder. It might take just a little longer. But you'd manage. Because nothing would be holding you back.

Natural Limitations?

It's easy enough to see how imaginary limitations can keep you from walking a plank across a chasm. It's easy enough to see how John's imaginary limitations might have prevented him ever landing a decent job as a salesman. But are *all* limitations of this type imaginary? We know that people are different. Surely it makes sense to suggest there must be some natural limitations beyond which an individual simply cannot go? This is a serious objection and deserves to be treated as such. The fact of the matter seems to be that while, theoretically, the human body and the human mind must have some *ultimate* limitations, you are very unlikely ever to reach them in practice—no matter how ambitious you become.

Let me give you an example of what I mean from the world of athletics. In the days of Queen Victoria, medical opinion was convinced that the idea of a man running a mile in four minutes was absurd. The limitations of the human body absolutely ruled this out. As the years went by, athletes pushed closer and closer to the ideal of the four-minute mile, but no matter how close they came, not even the best of them managed to break that magic barrier. Then along came Dr Roger Bannister. He was convinced the barrier really was 'magic'—in other words, that it existed entirely in the human mind. Nothing in his medical training had led him to believe it represented any ultimate barrier in terms of human physiology. He trained hard, believed in himself deeply, and eventually ran a sub-four-minute mile.

But, striking though Dr Bannister's achievement undoubtedly was, it remains far less impressive than what happened afterwards. For no sooner had Dr Bannister shown it could be done than scores of athletes were also suddenly able to run a mile in less than four minutes. Today, the sub-four-minute mile has become almost an athletic commonplace. Already the sights have been set on the three-and-a-half minute mile. And even this is unlikely to prove an ultimate barrier to athletes in the twenty-first century.

What happened here? One moment in time not a single athlete in the world could run a mile in four minutes. Another moment in time, and suddenly scores of men could do it. They still had the same bodies as before, the same hearts and muscles. They still had the same distance to run and the same time to run it in. They used the same old training methods and the same old running shoes. The difference was that one day they believed a sub-four-minute-mile impossible, while the next day Bannister proved them wrong. Suddenly they could imagine themselves duplicating his feat. And because they were able to imagine it, they were able to do it. Once Bannister showed the trick could actually be done, their imaginary limitations evaporated.

Almost everybody walks around with a vast burden of imaginary limitations inside their head. While the burden remains, personal success is as difficult to achieve as the conquest of Everest with a sack of rocks tied to your back. Bannister's four-minute mile was a striking example of how imaginary limitations can hold men back so firmly that they become convinced the limitations themselves are external realities — laws of nature which cannot be contravened. But it's not the only example.

Scientists have such a poor opinion of the human mind that in the 1950s they began to build machines to think for us. Today, computer technology has reached incredible heights of sophistication, and we stand in awe of the mathematical calculations these machines can perform. It seems insane to suggest the human brain could do better — yet there is any amount of proof that it can.

In the early eighteenth century, for example, an illiterate farm labourer from Derbyshire mentally calculated the result of doubling a farthing one hundred and thirty-nine times. His answer, checked by the use of logarithms, proved correct—even though, in £s, it ran to thirty-nine figures. This man—his name was Jedidiah Buxton—also memorized the number of words spoken by each actor appearing in Shakespeare's *Richard III*, plus the number of their exits and entrances. He managed this during a single performance; and it was the first time he had ever seen the play.

Zerah Colburn, an American farmer's son, was able to instantly calculate the number of seconds in 1,813 years, 7 months and 27 days (if you're curious, the answer is 57,234,384,000). The great Victorian engineer, George Bidder, was able to calculate the number of light waves striking the human eye in one second required to produce the effect of red—some 444,433,651,200,000. It took him only a second or two, without pencil and paper.

Cases like these make nonsense of the notion that the human mind is somehow naturally limited to the child's play it normally undertakes. The brains of Buxton, Colburn and Bidder were not substantially different from yours or mine (this is not a guess: time and again autopsies have been performed on mental prodigies in an attempt to find the secret of their skill. In every case there has been no abnormal brain development). How then were they able to perform feats which would baffle ordinary men?

It is a curious fact that most mental prodigies have come from highly unsophisticated backgrounds. They are poorly educated (or not educated at all) and surrounded by stupidity. They did not know—because no-one would have told them—that their minds should have been quite incapable of handling the prodigious calculations they did. In other words, in certain areas they had no imaginary limitations. Without them, they were more than a match for modern computers.

There are billions of cells in the human brain. Any neurologist will tell you we use only the merest fraction of them—a figure of 10% is usually quoted. Even the Einsteins amongst us do only marginally better. So, if it's your ambition to become as smart as Einstein, you're still limiting yourself needlessly. In theory, you could be *ten times* as smart as Einstein.

Maybe that's a little facetious, but it underlines the fact that, whatever your ambitions, you're unlikely *ever* to push up against any absolute limit of your potential. But as I've said before, you're very likely to push up against imaginary limitations. What can you do about this?

Stop Thinking About Limitations

The first step is to stop thinking that these limitations are a law of nature—something outside yourself. You must recognize them as imaginary. Things which exist only in your mind. Things which have been built up over a lifetime in ways you can clearly examine and chart (this is something I'll be dealing with in greater detail in the next chapter).

Next time you find yourself faced with a task you 'know' you can't do, take time to remember that what's stopping you isn't lack of ability, or talent, or even experience—but an imaginary limitation. The human mind is the oddest bag of tricks you'd ever meet with in a month of Sundays. The more you look inside it, the more you'd be convinced there was a little imp in there determined to hold people back from personal success, from personal satisfaction and happiness. And the incredible thing is, that little imp can hold you back with the weakest possible ropes—ropes that really don't have any substance at all once you examine them.

But the fact that a rope has no substance doesn't mean it can't tie you hand and foot. If you live in the country, you might like to try a novel—and very disturbing—experiment. Catch a hen, and hold its head down so that the beak touches the ground. Then, making sure the hen can see what you're doing, draw a firm chalk line from the beak along the ground. When the line is about a yard or two long, let go of the hen. The poor bird won't be able to straighten up. It's 'tied up' by the line you drew. This is, of course, an experiment in the realm of animal hypnosis. Hypnotic experiments on humans show we're just as susceptible to other types of mental ropes. Tell a subject in trance that he's met up with a brick wall, and he won't be able to take another step forward. More to the point, a post-hypnotic suggestion will ensure he still experiences the brick wall *after* he wakes up from trance. The wall may only exist in his mind, implanted by hypnotic suggestion, but it might as well be built with stones and mortar because there's no way he can walk through it.

Imaginary limitations are like that. In fact, they obey almost exactly the same psychological rules as hypnotic suggestions of the type I've just described. So while it's important to recognize your limitations as imaginary, that's only the first step. Simple realization of the situation is not enough.

We've already touched on this point earlier. Logic can tell you that the plank across the chasm is no more dangerous than the plank laid out on the ground. But that won't help you cross it. There's another example from the annals of hypnosis which illustrates this point as well. A London psychologist was experimenting with a colleague in the field of post-hypnotic suggestion. He told his subject under trance that, when given a particular keyword, he would feel compelled to get up and sit in a different chair. Then he woke the man up and subsequently gave the keyword. Now, the colleague was a man well experienced with the techniques of hypnosis. Although he didn't remember what had happened in trance, he was experienced enough to realize his sudden impulse had been triggered by a post-hypnotic suggestion. He told the psychologist that he had guessed the nature of the experiment and was determined to resist. But he couldn't. After a moment or two of internal struggle, he got up and sat on the other chair. Realization of the situation was not enough.

In the next chapter, I'll be showing you the way to see your imaginary limitations clearly. Once they're out in the open, I'll be asking you to examine each of them coolly, so that you can see for yourself they exist only in your own head and in no way represent external laws of nature. In the chapter after that, we'll put our heads together to find out where your imaginary limitations come from, how they were built up and how they form a composite image of yourself which *simply is not true*.

But all this will be absolutely useless to you unless you have the secret of breaking down those imaginary limitations. Until that happens, you're no better off than the psychologist's colleague who knew what was going on, but couldn't stop himself switching chairs; or the hypnotic subject who can see perfectly well that there is no wall in front of him, but still can't walk through it. We'll be going into all this in depth a little later. And as we do, you'll learn several tried and tested techniques which have been used by others — myself included — in order to render imaginary limitations harmless.

But even before we reach that point, I'd like to give you what I call the *vital secret*. I'm giving it to you now because you're interested in personal success (otherwise you wouldn't be reading this book), and people interested in personal success are people in a hurry. The *vital secret* is this:

SINCE IMAGINATION PUT YOUR LIMITATIONS UP THERE IN THE FIRST PLACE, IMAGINATION IS THE THING TO USE TO TAKE THEM DOWN AGAIN.

2

A Place To Stand

The ancient Greek Archimedes was the first man on Earth to discover the principle of the lever, by which a man might move weights out of all proportion to his physical strength. Archimedes was so intrigued by the lever that he claimed he could use it to move the world . . . if he had a place to stand.

You are, at this moment, in a very similar situation. Given a place to stand, you could move the entire business world—with results out of all proportion to the effort applied. The problem, as with Archimedes, is the place to stand.

It's true you have a place to stand at the moment. That's to say you have a psychological base of operations. But probably you're not really very much aware of it. You have a hazy idea of your strengths and weaknesses, but the chances are you haven't really thought about either in any real detail. You've just acted—or failed to act—on certain semi-conscious, or totally unconscious assumptions about yourself. I want to tell you here and now that most, if not all, of those assumptions are wrong. And if you make use of the techniques explained later in this book, they'll change . . . for the better. But that's moving ahead of things. For the moment, the important task is to find out *exactly* where you stand in relation to yourself. In the next chapter, we'll have a closer look at where this stance comes from, how it was built up. At present, however, all we have to do is examine it.

In order to do this, I want you to complete the quiz that

follows. I want you to complete it right here in this book. Maybe you're like me and don't like writing in books, but I'd like you to put that distaste to one side and write in this one. There's a reason. The quiz is not only designed to show you where you stand in relation to yourself now, it's also designed as a yardstick. In the weeks and months ahead, you will be going over the quiz again and again. If you've been practising *Power Play* techniques in the interim, you're going to find your answers have changed — and in some cases changed drastically. And as your answers change, your final score will change. By comparing your new scores with your original scores, you will have a very accurate measure of your progress.

And that's the reason why I want you to do the quiz *now*. If you wait until you've practised even one of the Power Play techniques, you won't get an accurate base reading. This is an important point, so you'll forgive me if I stress it: DO THE QUIZ NOW. BEFORE READING ANY OTHER CHAPTER OF THIS BOOK.

There are some things you should know about the quiz before you start. The first is, you should keep your answers secret. Show them to nobody. Not to your parents, not to your wife, not to your children, relatives or friends. Absolute secrecy is the rule. If you have to, lock this book up in a safe after you've completed the quiz. In any case, make absolutely sure nobody will ever know your answers. The reason for this is that you must answer every question in the quiz with *scrupulous honesty*. In some cases this will be very difficult, because the questions are very personal and probing. But if somebody else is likely to look at your answers, the job won't be just difficult — it'll be downright impossible. The unconscious mind is a funny thing, and it's going to influence your answers if it thinks there's a chance of somebody else seeing them. Instead of answering just for yourself, you'll unconsciously be answering for somebody else. You'll try subtly to improve things just a little so you won't look so bad to the person who's going to read the score. And that means your result is going to be inaccurate.

The next thing you should know is this quiz doesn't have any right or wrong answers. This probably makes it a lot different from any quiz you've ever tried before. It isn't even like those psychological evaluation tests where you have to choose between two positions. Even though they *say* there's no right answer in these tests, anyone with half an ounce of intelligence can usually guess which choice is going to show him up in the better light.

But our present quiz isn't like that at all. Because it's not designed to show the sort of person you are. It's designed to show the sort of person you *think* you are. And there's a big difference.

Now let's get on to the quiz itself. It's pretty long, but try if you can to work all the way through it in a single session. If you can't, don't worry—it's not vital; but do try to come back and complete it as soon as possible.

Answer every question. If the question refers to a situation you aren't in at the moment, or have never been in at any time in the past, try to imagine how you'd act in that situation and give an answer anyway. Don't spend a lot of time on any question, trying to make up your mind about the answer. Remember, the quiz is designed to let you know how you see yourself, not how you are. So the first answer that comes into your head is probably the most accurate one you'll ever get. Put it down, then move on to the next question.

Okay, let's get started.

SELF IMAGE QUIZ

Instructions:

1. Tackle every question quickly and honestly.
2. The quiz is composed of evaluation questions. You are asked to mark yourself on a scale which ranges from zero to 10 in each case. For ease of marking, the scale is printed after each question. Simply put a circle round the figure which best expresses your evaluation.

Example:

Let's suppose you are faced with the question, 'How good are you at handling people? 0, 1, 2, 3, 4, 5, 6, 7, 8, 9, 10.'

If you ring the zero it means you consider yourself absolutely useless at handling people. You see yourself as somebody who may be able to take orders, but certainly can't give them effectively.

If you ring 5, then you consider yourself about average at handling people, no better or worse than most, because 5 comes exactly half way along the scale.

If you ring 10, then it means you consider yourself absolutely expert at handling people. You are convinced you have nothing to learn on the subject and, whatever else your failings may be, the ability to handle people is not amongst them.

In all probability, you might pick some other number on the scale. If you pick 1, it would mean you consider yourself well below average in handling people, but not absolutely useless. If you picked 9, then you consider yourself well above average, but not perfect. And so on.

When you've completed the quiz, I'll tell you how to score.

Section A: Childhood Background

1. How well did you get on with your father up to the time you were eight years old? 0, 1, 2, 3, 4, 5, 6, 7, 8, 9, 10.

2. How well did you get on with your mother up to the time you were eight years old? 0, 1, 2, 3, 4, 5, 6, 7, 8, 9, 10.

3. Counting yourself, your parents and any brothers or sisters, how many members were in your family up to your ninth birthday? (If more than 10, ring 10). 1, 2, 3, 4, 5, 6, 7, 8, 9, 10.

(NOTE: Orphans should answer questions 1 and 2 in relation to those adult(s) who took the closest personal hand in their upbringing. If either of your parents died before you were four years old score zero against the question relating to that parent.)

4. Generally speaking, how popular were you with your schoolmates at Primary School? 0, 1, 2, 3, 4, 5, 6, 7, 8, 9, 10.

5. And how popular were you with your Primary School teachers? 0, 1, 2, 3, 4, 5, 6, 7, 8, 9, 10.

6. How bright a child were you up to the age of eight? 0, 1, 2, 3, 4, 5, 6, 7, 8, 9, 10.

7. How did you do in games and sports? 0, 1, 2, 3, 4, 5, 6, 7, 8, 9, 10.

8. Again up to the age of eight, do you consider you were particularly imaginative? 0, 1, 2, 3, 4, 5, 6, 7, 8, 9, 10.

9. Do you feel your childhood was a happy one? 0, 1, 2, 3, 4, 5, 6, 7, 8, 9, 10.

10. Were you a healthy child? 0, 1, 2, 3, 4, 5, 6, 7, 8, 9, 10.

11. How well loved were you as a child? 0, 1, 2, 3, 4, 5, 6, 7, 8, 9, 10.

Section B: Adolescence

12. During adolescence how popular were you with members of the opposite sex? 0, 1, 2, 3, 4, 5, 6, 7, 8, 9, 10.

13. How good-looking were you? 0, 1, 2, 3, 4, 5, 6, 7, 8, 9, 10.

14. How individualistic were you? 0, 1, 2, 3, 4, 5, 6, 7, 8, 9, 10.

Section C: Current Attitudes

15. Are you ambitious? 0, 1, 2, 3, 4, 5, 6, 7, 8, 9, 10.

16. Do you consider yourself intelligent? 0, 1, 2, 3, 4, 5, 6, 7, 8, 9, 10.

17. Have you a strong personality? 0, 1, 2, 3, 4, 5, 6, 7, 8, 9, 10.

18. How decisive are you? 0, 1, 2, 3, 4, 5, 6, 7, 8, 9, 10.

19. How much charm do you feel you have? 0, 1, 2, 3, 4, 5, 6, 7, 8, 9, 10.

20. Are you sexually attractive? 0, 1, 2, 3, 4, 5, 6, 7, 8, 9, 10.

21. How do you measure up in ability against colleagues in your own field? 0, 1, 2, 3, 4, 5, 6, 7, 8, 9, 10.

22. Do you have leadership potential? 0, 1, 2, 3, 4, 5, 6, 7, 8, 9, 10.

23. Do you enjoy taking risks? 0, 1, 2, 3, 4, 5, 6, 7, 8, 9, 10.

24. Are you aggressive? 0, 1, 2, 3, 4, 5, 6, 7, 8, 9, 10.

25. Do you consider yourself brave? 0, 1, 2, 3, 4, 5, 6, 7, 8, 9, 10.

26. Are you healthy? 0, 1, 2, 3, 4, 5, 6, 7, 8, 9, 10.

27. How would you rate your general levels of energy? 0, 1, 2, 3, 4, 5, 6, 7, 8, 9, 10.

28. Generally speaking, how happy are you? 0, 1, 2, 3, 4, 5, 6, 7, 8, 9, 10.

29. Do you find it easy to relax? 0, 1, 2, 3, 4, 5, 6, 7, 8, 9, 10.

30. How do you rate your memory? 0, 1, 2, 3, 4, 5, 6, 7, 8, 9, 10.

31. How efficient are you? 0, 1, 2, 3, 4, 5, 6, 7, 8, 9, 10.

32. How strong are your powers of concentration? 0, 1, 2, 3, 4, 5, 6, 7, 8, 9, 10.

33. Do you consider yourself lucky? 0, 1, 2, 3, 4, 5, 6, 7, 8, 9, 10.

34. Are you at ease with members of your own sex? 0, 1, 2, 3, 4, 5, 6, 7, 8, 9, 10.

35. Are you at ease with members of the opposite sex? 0, 1, 2, 3, 4, 5, 6, 7, 8, 9, 10.

36. If you were marooned in a strange city with neither friends nor money how well do you think you would cope? 0, 1, 2, 3, 4, 5, 6, 7, 8, 9, 10.

37. If you were marooned on an island with lots of game and fruit but no dangerous animals, and your only weapon was a knife, how well do you think you would survive? 0, 1, 2, 3, 4, 5, 6, 7, 8, 9, 10.

38. How about if there *were* dangerous animals? 0, 1, 2, 3, 4, 5, 6, 7, 8, 9, 10.

39. Finally, how would you feel if there were dangerous animals, game, but no fruit? 0, 1, 2, 3, 4, 5, 6, 7, 8, 9, 10.

40. How much do you enjoy your own company? 0, 1, 2, 3, 4, 5, 6, 7, 8, 9, 10.

41. How much do you fancy making a parachute jump? 0, 1, 2, 3, 4, 5, 6, 7, 8, 9, 10.

42. How do you rate your chances of surviving more than a few days on a raft, without food, in the middle of the Atlantic? 0, 1, 2, 3, 4, 5, 6, 7, 8, 9, 10.

43. Rate the success chances of any company you might form. 0, 1, 2, 3, 4, 5, 6, 7, 8, 9, 10.

44. Do you feel you have better business sense than most? 0, 1, 2, 3, 4, 5, 6, 7, 8, 9, 10.

45. Are you intuitive? 0, 1, 2, 3, 4, 5, 6, 7, 8, 9, 10.

46. Do people like you? 0, 1, 2, 3, 4, 5, 6, 7, 8, 9, 10.

47. Do you consider yourself physically fit? 0, 1, 2, 3, 4, 5, 6, 7, 8, 9, 10.

48. Are you physically well-proportioned? 0, 1, 2, 3, 4, 5, 6, 7, 8, 9, 10.

49. Do you have good skin? 0, 1, 2, 3, 4, 5, 6, 7, 8, 9, 10.

50. How well pleased are you with the way you look? 0, 1, 2, 3, 4, 5, 6, 7, 8, 9, 10.

51. How about the way you dress? 0, 1, 2, 3, 4, 5, 6, 7, 8, 9, 10.

52. How tenacious are you? 0, 1, 2, 3, 4, 5, 6, 7, 8, 9, 10.

53. How well can you work within a team? 0, 1, 2, 3, 4, 5, 6, 7, 8, 9, 10.

54. Do you feel yourself a persuasive individual? 0, 1, 2, 3, 4, 5, 6, 7, 8, 9, 10.

55. If you were running a business team, how well could you cope with an out and out trouble-maker? 0, 1, 2, 3, 4, 5, 6, 7, 8, 9, 10.

56. You hire your best friend for an important post in your company. He turns out to be useless. How easy would it be

for you to fire him? 0, 1, 2, 3, 4, 5, 6, 7, 8, 9, 10.

57. How good a job do you think you would make of running the United States? 0, 1, 2, 3, 4, 5, 6, 7, 8, 9, 10.

58. How about running a multi-national corporation? 0, 1, 2, 3, 4, 5, 6, 7, 8, 9, 10.

59. How well do you feel you manage personal relationships with people of the same sex? 0, 1, 2, 3, 4, 5, 6, 7, 8, 9, 10.

60. And with people of the opposite sex? 0, 1, 2, 3, 4, 5, 6, 7, 8, 9, 10.

61. How well do you repair things about the house? 0, 1, 2, 3, 4, 5, 6, 7, 8, 9, 10.

62. How self-sufficient are you? 0, 1, 2, 3, 4, 5, 6, 7, 8, 9, 10.

63. If you were required to make a speech before 2,000 university graduates, how well do you think you'd handle it? 0, 1, 2, 3, 4, 5, 6, 7, 8, 9, 10.

64. Can you write memos well? 0, 1, 2, 3, 4, 5, 6, 7, 8, 9, 10.

65. How adequate do you feel your educational background has been? 0, 1, 2, 3, 4, 5, 6, 7, 8, 9, 10.

66. Generally speaking, how well do you rate your powers of discernment? 0, 1, 2, 3, 4, 5, 6, 7, 8, 9, 10.

67. And how about discrimination? 0, 1, 2, 3, 4, 5, 6, 7, 8, 9, 10.

68. What level of good taste have you? 0, 1, 2, 3, 4, 5, 6, 7, 8, 9, 10.

69. How would you rate your level of sophistication? 0, 1, 2, 3, 4, 5, 6, 7, 8, 9, 10.

70. Are you a good driver? 0, 1, 2, 3, 4, 5, 6, 7, 8, 9, 10.

71. Rate your financial potential? 0, 1, 2, 3, 4, 5, 6, 7, 8, 9, 10.

72. Do you feel you are currently living up to this potential? 0, 1, 2, 3, 4, 5, 6, 7, 8, 9, 10.

73. How strongly do you feel members of the opposite sex are

attracted to you? 0, 1, 2, 3, 4, 5, 6, 7, 8, 9, 10.

74. How do you rate your physical reaction time? 0, 1, 2, 3, 4, 5, 6, 7, 8, 9, 10.

75. How well and quickly do you react *mentally* to an unexpected situation? 0, 1, 2, 3, 4, 5, 6, 7, 8, 9, 10.

76. How cool are you in a crisis? 0, 1, 2, 3, 4, 5, 6, 7, 8, 9, 10.

77. Do you consider yourself well-read? 0, 1, 2, 3, 4, 5, 6, 7, 8, 9, 10.

78. Do you sleep well? 0, 1, 2, 3, 4, 5, 6, 7, 8, 9, 10.

79. How high up the social ladder do you see yourself at present? 0, 1, 2, 3, 4, 5, 6, 7, 8, 9, 10.

80. Do you believe yourself well-travelled? 0, 1, 2, 3, 4, 5, 6, 7, 8, 9, 10.

81. You're forced to take a job as a door to door salesman of brushes. How well do you think you'd fare? 0, 1, 2, 3, 4, 5, 6, 7, 8, 9, 10.

82. You've landed a job selling executive aeroplanes to an international business market. How well do you think you'd fare? 0, 1, 2, 3, 4, 5, 6, 7, 8, 9, 10.

83. You have to escort a glamorous film star (of the opposite sex) on a night out in your city. How confident are you of giving him/her an interesting time? 0, 1, 2, 3, 4, 5, 6, 7, 8, 9, 10.

84. You've netted a job as a night-club 'bouncer' in a tough district. How well will you handle it? 0, 1, 2, 3, 4, 5, 6, 7, 8, 9, 10.

85. You have to entertain world chess champ Bobbie Fischer for an hour without once mentioning chess. How well would you fare? 0, 1, 2, 3, 4, 5, 6, 7, 8, 9, 10.

86. What do you feel is your potential as a chess master? 0, 1, 2, 3, 4, 5, 6, 7, 8, 9, 10.

87. What do you feel is your potential as a kung-fu master? 0, 1, 2, 3, 4, 5, 6, 7, 8, 9, 10.

88. What level of interest have you in exotic foods? 0, 1, 2, 3, 4, 5, 6, 7, 8, 9, 10.

89. How well do you manage money? 0, 1, 2, 3, 4, 5, 6, 7, 8, 9, 10.

90. Rate your level of self-confidence. 0, 1, 2, 3, 4, 5, 6, 7, 8, 9, 10.

91. Do you cook well? 0, 1, 2, 3, 4, 5, 6, 7, 8, 9, 10.

92. What's your level of musical appreciation? 0, 1, 2, 3, 4, 5, 6, 7, 8, 9, 10.

93. If you felt like singing aloud about the house, how likely are you actually to do so? 0, 1, 2, 3, 4, 5, 6, 7, 8, 9, 10.

94. What do you feel are the chances of life after death? 0, 1, 2, 3, 4, 5, 6, 7, 8, 9, 10.

95. What do you feel are your chances of making a million? 0, 1, 2, 3, 4, 5, 6, 7, 8, 9, 10.

96. How tough, psychologically, do you reckon you are? 0, 1, 2, 3, 4, 5, 6, 7, 8, 9, 10.

97. If your country's entire political and economic system were overthrown overnight in a revolution, how do you rate your chances of finding your feet quickly and prospering under the new regime? 0, 1, 2, 3, 4, 5, 6, 7, 8, 9, 10.

98. How much do you know about the human mind? 0, 1, 2, 3, 4, 5, 6, 7, 8, 9, 10.

99. You have made an honest mistake which cost your company £50,000. You are called to a Board meeting to explain. How well do you think you'd do? 0, 1, 2, 3, 4, 5, 6, 7, 8, 9, 10.

100. Do you feel competent to advise nuclear scientists on the morality of creating bigger bombs? 0, 1, 2, 3, 4, 5, 6, 7, 8, 9, 10.

That's the worst of it over. Now let's see how you scored. Go back over the quiz and add up all the numbers you've

POSITIVE PERCENTAGE CHART

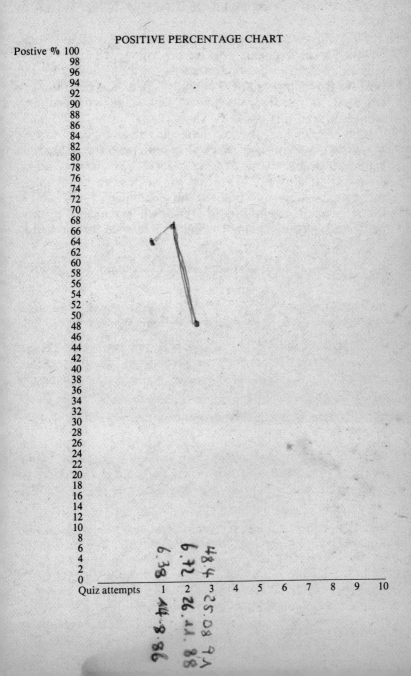

Postive % 100
98
96
94
92
90
88
86
84
82
80
78
76
74
72
70
68
66
64
62
60
58
56
54
52
50
48
46
44
42
40
38
36
34
32
30
28
26
24
22
20
18
16
14
12
10
8
6
4
2
0

Quiz attempts   1   2   3   4   5   6   7   8   9   10

ringed. When you've done that, divide your final answer by 10.

This will give you your *positive percentage* in self-image terms. The higher your positive percentage, the more likely you are to achieve personal success. But don't worry if your positive percentage is low. I actually expect it to be low at this stage. If it wasn't pretty low at this stage, you probably wouldn't need this book.

And high or low, the techniques in this book can improve it, In fact, so you can check this statement for yourself, I want you to mark your positive percentage right now on the simple chart above. Then after you've read this book right through and started to practise the techniques, I want you to take the quiz again and mark down your new positive percentage. You're going to find a difference for the better.

3

Improving Your Place

Obviously I don't know how you scored. But I do know one thing. You didn't score highly enough. No matter how honest you thought you were, no matter how objective you thought you were, you didn't score highly enough.

Nearly every question in that quiz is concerned with qualities which go to make up a success person. Qualities like self-sufficiency, toughness, intelligence, fitness, resilience, imagination, personality, honesty. I *know* you have those qualities. I *know* you have everything inside you that's necessary for your success. How do I know? Because the study of psychology—practical, applied psychology—used to be my full time job (and still is, in a way). And during the time I worked in this field, I discovered something very interesting. I discovered that what holds people back isn't lack of talent, isn't lack of 'success qualities' like intelligence, resilience or personality. What holds people back is lack of confidence. And that, in turn, springs from their imaginary limitations. That's how I know you didn't score highly enough. Because everyone lacks confidence in certain fields. Everyone in some respect is a prey to imaginary limitations. Put too many of those imaginary limitations together, and you've got something called a *negative self image*.

Your Self Image
We've already skirted round this question of self image.

Now's the time to look at it a bit more closely.

Psychology is still a long way from discovering what makes people the way they are. Some schools of thought figure you were born with a mind like a sort of blank slate or empty book. As you grew up, your environment—the things, people and situations around you—filled up the book, made you what you are today. According to this school of thought, what you are today is no more than a collection of previous experiences which condition your outlook, personality and reactions. Psychologists who believe this theory are called Behaviourists. They feel a human being can be totally summed up in terms of how he behaves.

Another school of psychological thought says you weren't born with a blank slate in your head after all. Instead, you entered this world nicely equipped with a whole host of inherited characteristics. These determine how you will react to situations right through your life.

Maybe, as yet another school teaches, the truth lies somewhere between the two of these extremes. But right now we're less concerned with what makes you the way you are than with what makes you *think* you are a certain way. The fact is, very few people see themselves clearly. You've certainly noticed this among your friends. How often have you met a man who was completely blind to his own faults, even when they were pointed out to him by others? And just as often, you'll meet people blind to their own good points as well. Frequently you'll meet people who think themselves to be the exact opposite of what they are. A brave man might consider himself a coward. A fool might think himself wise . . . and the wisest of men almost always think themselves fools.

Psychologists use the term 'image', or 'self-image' to describe the way we see ourselves. And, as we've already noted, your self-image doesn't have to bear the slightest resemblance to what you really are. In fact, most of this book is based on the assumption that your self-image is almost completely wrong.

If this is true, you might wonder how on earth it came about. After all, you can probably sum up other people accurately enough. Even if you're not a particularly good judge of character on first impressions, experience soon shows you if a man is a hero or a villain, a sage or a fool. In these circumstances, you might feel it odd that you could be so wrong about the most important person in your life—yourself. And it's even more odd when you stop to consider that, theoretically, you have a better chance of knowing yourself than anybody else. You live with yourself twenty-four hours a day. You are aware of your most secret actions. You even know what you are thinking. So how is it possible your self-image could be so far off the mark?

It's possible for a very unexpected reason. Your self-image *was not formed by you*. Furthermore, it was not formed *of* you.

That sounds very contradictory and confusing. But it will soon become clear. To get to the bottom of the mystery, you have to go back to childhood. From the day you were born (maybe even before) to about the age of eight, you were in your formative years. One of the things that was being formed was your self-image. Most of the work was done early, in the first three or four years, but until you were eight, things were still plastic enough to allow changes to take place. After that it got harder, although the massive glandular and psychological changes in adolescence would also tend to give a bit of elbow room for self-image changing, to some degree at least. But once adolescence was finished, once you became an adult, the self-image set like cement. For better or worse you thought you knew what you were, and only a pretty determined effort is about to change it.

The Formative Years

Let's examine those years when the basic pattern of your self-image was formed. You're under four years old, little more than a baby. To use an American expression, you don't know nuttin' from nuttin'. You are looking out at a big wide world around you, and none of it makes sense. Furthermore, none of it *can* make sense—you simply haven't developed the necessary intellectual equipment to sort out the sheep from the goats. Everything you know is fed in from outside. Most of it comes from your parents (particularly your mother), your brothers and your sisters. A little comes from casual acquaintances, more distant relatives and friends. You accept this information as accurate because you've nothing to compare it with; you haven't the experience to decide whether something's true or not. And the type of information fed in at this time plays a big part in developing your self-image. Were you a good boy or a bad boy? Were you smart or slow? Were you pretty or ugly—or just pretty ugly? Were you a help about the house, or just a little nuisance? Were you an interesting little lad, talked to and admired, or a child seen and not heard, and therefore boring?

You got the answers to all these questions from the people around you. And very often they were negative answers. Compared to an adult, young children are stupid, irritating and frequently dull. Maybe that was the feeling fed into you at that time. As a result, you began to feel yourself less bright than others, less skilful, less talented, more clumsy, less interesting. Things were probably easier if you had brothers or sisters around your own age, because the gap between your abilities and theirs would have been slightly less alarming. But only slightly.

Apart from the information fed in, you were faced, in those early days, with an incontrovertible fact of life. You were little and you were powerless. This is an aspect of childhood very quickly forgotten in adult years. Subjects under hypnotic regression (which brings back vivid memories of childhood) are often astonished to find how gigantic the furniture has grown. But the furniture hasn't grown at all—it's their viewpoint that has shrunk.

The experience of being small and helpless was so pronounced, so dramatic, so consistent, that it became a cornerstone of your self-image. Even with the most loving, most understanding environment in the world, you still saw yourself as weak and ineffectual . . . because that's exactly what you were. This was reinforced (again even in the most loving, caring environment) by the fact that most of the things you naturally wanted to do were socially unacceptable. You were taught that passing waste when you needed to—the most natural thing in the world from a subjective viewpoint—was wrong. If you attempted to explore the interesting texture of that waste, you were suddenly 'dirty'. If you wanted food and your timing didn't suit those whose job it was to get it for you, you were told to wait. As you grew a little older and tried to assert your own authority on the world—a deeply felt need in any powerless individual—you were very quickly put back in your place. Thus, layer by layer, your self-image began to grow. Small . . . helpless . . . powerless . . . dirty . . . socially unacceptable . . . inferior. You didn't think of it in those terms, of course, but that's basically how you saw yourself and that's basically how you were.

By the time you were ready to step out into the world—to go to nursery school, perhaps—you'd probably corrected the worst of these faults. You had pretty good control of bladder and bowel; and if you were hungry, you now had enough power to grab yourself a hunk of bread. And even if you weren't as big as an adult, you felt you were a lot bigger than you had been.

The trouble was, nobody gave you very much credit for these massive achievements. Instead of pats on the back and a well-earned rest on your laurels, you were being spurred on to conquer newer, vaster, more esoteric heights—like learning to read and write, or use the right knife at the dinner table. So even your achievements didn't do much for your self-image. Deep down, you still felt basically small, helpless, powerless, dirty, socially unacceptable and inferior. And once again, this self-image was basically accurate. In an adult world, young children tend to be all these things. Naturally, this does not reflect the slightest discredit on the child; but it is an accurate expression of the way things are.

At this stage you went to school, and had your first major confrontation with dozens of other children facing the same problems you did and reacting to them in a variety of different ways. But behind the variety was a common pattern: the need to establish superiority as widely as possible. But because of the age spectrum in any primary school—running from about five to about twelve—older children really were superior. Once more your self-image received negative reinforcement.

And all this presupposes a trauma-free childhood!

As Freudian psychiatrists have discovered, few childhoods are entirely trauma-free. Parents are only human, and behave badly at times, even towards their children. Love and affection are not always there when a child needs them. Understanding is frequently lacking. Sympathy is often absent. Because childhood experiences are essentially painful, they are quickly forgotten—another psychological mechanism, this. And because they have forgotten, adults rarely understand a child's needs.

As you continue to grow, however, the first real possibility of a positive self-image begins to emerge. By the time you are seven or eight, you have a considerable amount of control over your environment. You can walk properly. You have a very considerable vocabulary. You can read and write quite well enough to absorb and pass on quite sophisticated information. You are taller and stronger and more tightly co-ordinated. You have developed sufficiently in the intellectual sphere to allow you to compare your achievements with those of your peers, rather than with those of adults. You have greatly increased mobility, for while you cannot drive a car, you can at least ride a bike.

The 'Nightmare' of Adolescence

At this stage, given an essentially benevolent environment, you may well begin to lay down a few positive layers on your self-image. But time is short, for by the age of eight the image has virtually solidified; and while the thin outer layers may be positive, the heart of the onion is pretty rotten. With this unfortunate equipment, you plunge gaily into the nightmare of adolescence.

Nightmare's not too strong a word. Your world, which was just beginning to show some measure of security, is suddenly turned upside down. No-one will accept you as an adult, but you have lost interest in childish pursuits. Your appearance has become terribly important for the first time in your life; and for the first time in your life you are a mass of spots and pimples. You are seized by the most violent of emotional urges which you have little or no opportunity to do anything about. It is vital to convince those around you that you know everything, yet at heart you realize you know nothing.

If there is one word which ably describes adolescence, that word is confusion. And the confusion is so strongly felt that it can easily impinge on your basic self-image. It's a sorry picture: small . . . helpless . . . powerless . . . dirty . . . socially unacceptable . . . inferior . . . confused—and, in particularly bad cases, unloved and unwanted as well. And sorry though it is, the image was largely accurate when it was laid down— not by yourself, but by the actions and opinions of others.

And at this stage, Nature played you the dirtiest trick imaginable. You grew up, but your self-image didn't.

For centuries philosophers have talked about the 'human condition'. They've wondered why men behave the way they do, wondered why so many people are so hard on themselves and on others. I don't pretend I've found the answer to the mystery of the human condition, but I do know that Nature's dirty trick has done a great deal to mess things up for an awful lot of people. Think about it for a minute and you'll see it stands to reason. The picture I've painted of the way a negative self-image is built up doesn't include obscure psychological terms or abstract concepts of the mind. But it does include a lot of common sense. You can see easily and clearly not just that a negative self-image is likely to arise, but that it's almost certain to arise.

You can also see it's likely to arise in everybody; not just those poor unfortunates with a deprived and difficult childhood (although a difficult childhood will obviously exaggerate the problem).

As the years go by, most people learn to bury the worst aspects of their self-image. But a thing that's buried isn't necessarily destroyed. So that, deep down, those old feelings of worthlessness, powerlessness, social unacceptability and the rest are still there. Occasionally they will reach out to overpower you for a time, bringing those barren periods that even the most optimistic personality sometimes experiences, when life seems absolutely futile and all his efforts are in vain.

The neurotic is in an even worse state, for his negative self-image is turned inside out. Instead of the rotten layers being well buried under a positive skin, he senses them on the surface, making him feel powerless, worthless and inferior all the time. This is the frightening power of the negative self-image. It's purely a mental construction. It was laid down, by others, when you were a child and couldn't sort the nonsense from the truth. It pays no attention whatsoever to the patent fact that you're no longer the same being you were at the age of one or two. Your self-image turns a blind eye to the fact that you're now eating steak and chips, not surviving on your mother's milk. Your self-image presents you with a picture of yourself as a child. And while you'd never mistake that tousle-headed picture in the family album for the man you are today, the fact that the self-image is largely unconscious means you will frequently accept the picture it presents, however wildly out of date.

Tackling Your Negative Self-Image

Mental or not, unconscious or semi-conscious, the negative self-image is an amazingly strong construction. Left alone, it will endure a lifetime. And it is the fertile soil in which imaginary limitations take root. The proverb has it that what goes up must come down—a saying which admittedly fails to take into account peculiarities like hydrogen baloons. But it is perfectly true to say (in the light of experience) that any psychological construction can be taken down.

It is not, however, true to say it can be taken down easily. Psychological constructions are a bit like buildings. The more modern ones among them tend to be flimsy, and come apart easily. The older structures seem to be far more solidly built. In the negative self-image, we are dealing with a very old structure and one that has to be tackled with a fair degree of skill if we are to get anywhere with demolishing it.

People tend to get very excited when they first realize the truth about their negative self-image. They think that, now that they recognize it as a description of the way they were in childhood, bearing no relation to the way they are today, it will somehow go away. It's as well to quash that rumour here and now. While recognizing your self-image for what it really is may be a step in the right direction, it's not the whole journey by any means. You're going to have to take my word for that for the moment—and take it against some pretty heavy opposition. Freudian psychologists, for instance, have a theory that if you bring something up from the unconscious and examine it rationally, it loses much of its effectiveness and power. I don't know if I believe that theory at all, but I certainly don't believe it in relation to a negative self-image. You can make up your mind. You now know how your self-image was built up. Does that mean you suddenly feel you could take on the world? If it doesn't, don't despair. There are ways and means to change a self-image. And once the process starts, it's like a snowball rolling downhill. In psychological terms, the process is self-reinforcing. You'll learn from personal experience exactly what that means a little later on.

In the meantime, I want to say a word or two which may save you a lot of time, may stop you running down a few of the more inviting blind alleys.

The first thing I want to say is that experience won't change your negative self-image. No matter how often you succeed as an adult, no matter how many tasks you accomplish, no matter how much people like or admire you, it won't change your negative self-image one iota. This may sound as if I've suddenly turned against the idea of success. I haven't. But I've no time at all for success without happiness. What's the point of making a million if you can't enjoy it? What's the point of reaching the top slot in your company if you're not happy there? The royal road to real success starts by working from the inside out, by getting your head into shape before you tackle the jobs around you.

The next thing I want to say is that the negative self-image is utterly impervious to logic. It wasn't constructed logically, and it's not about to be broken down logically either.

The final thing is that common sense is not enough either—although common sense will help. You may know it's silly to see yourself as you were when you were a child. Common sense tells you it's silly. And so long as you're facing that squarely, it helps. But you won't be able to face it squarely every waking minute of the day—you've other, better things to do. And once your attention slips, that old negative self-image will start exercising its destructive influence again, subtly but strongly.

All of which sounds a lot more depressing than it's meant to be. Because you *can* change your self-image. You can change it permanently. You can change it dramatically. You can pull down that old building brick by brick. What's even better news, you can start the job the minute you've finished reading the next chapter.

4

The Lazy First Steps To Success

When I practised as a hypnotherapist, I treated dozens of patients who were 'locked in' to their personal problems. Typically, they would find themselves at a sort of emotional turning point, but felt themselves to be stuck—unable to go forward, unable to go back. There was usually an obvious answer to their problem, an obvious course of action. They could see it easily, but it was always a course they felt they 'couldn't' take. Thus, unable to endure the problem, and unable to take the relevant steps to solve it, they found themselves locked in a painful position.

I had one question I put to every one of these patients. The question was this: *who makes your rules?*

Work at the clinic fairly quickly convinced me that everyone lives their lives in strict accordance with a rigid set of rules. The rules themselves vary from person to person. Some people have a lot. Some people have a few. But the rules are always there.

There are three different types of rule. The first type describes the sort of thing you *must not*, or *cannot* do. For example, this type of rule might insist you must never, under any circumstances, deceive a friend. Thus, deceiving a friend becomes something you could not do. The second type describes the sort of thing you *must* do. This might be something as simple as taking a bath every day. Or always keeping at least £100 in a savings account. Or tidying your own desk, rather than letting your secretary near it. The third type of rule is a lot more subtle. This rule describes *how things should be*. One patient of mine was in enormous emotional difficulties because her boy-friend, who said he loved her, did not behave like a man in love. In other words, my patient carried round a rule in her head which described how a man in love should behave.

All these rules have a tendency to operate below the level of consciousness. They are never examined, analysed, or questioned. But they are enormously strong for all that. In many cases they are totally unbreakable.

You carry a complete set of rules around in your head at this moment. I don't know what they are, of course, but that's not important. What *is* important is the probability that you don't know either. Until now, you probably didn't even think of them as rules. They were just a part of your personality, or a part of the way the world is. But they aren't part of your personality, and they aren't part of the way the world is. They're rules somebody made up for you and planted firmly in your head.

Who Made Your Rules?

Some of them were undoubtedly made by you. Not many, but some. Most of them were made by other people. Your parents made quite a lot—probably the majority. Your relatives and friends added to the total. There may even be a few in there made by the television set or the books you read. None of this would necessarily be a bad thing if every rule in your set was a good rule. But there's no guarantee this is the case. Patients who came to me for therapy were suffering from their rules. Their rules actually prevented them from living full and happy lives. And the wrong rules can stop you dead on the road to personal success.

Right now you're going to take the first step down that road. It's a lazy man's step because you won't even have to get up from your comfortable armchair. Here's what I want you to do:

Close your eyes and think about your rules.

You won't be able to think about them as rules, of course. Even after what I've told you, they're still going to feel like something different. So instead of looking round in your head for a set of rules all written down and neat, I want you to think about courses of action you know you could never take.

Start with something pretty obvious and exaggerated. We both know you could never murder your granny or rob a bank (at least I *hope* we both know that). Okay, so that's one of your obvious rules. Where did it come from? Not from you, I'm prepared to bet. You never actually sat down one day and said to yourself, 'Should I or should I not murder my granny?' You never looked consciously into the pros and cons. You never made a hard decision, based on logic, that granny murder wasn't on.

So if it didn't come from you, where did it come from? My guess is it came from your parents. Maybe even when they were teaching you the Ten Commandments. *Thou shalt not kill*. And that obviously includes grannies.

So now you know one of your rules and where it came from. Is it a good rule, or a bad rule? Maybe granny will leave you that antique lamp you've always wanted. Is that a good reason for murder? Hardly. And if you do slip arsenic in her gin, there's every chance the police will find you out. Do you want to spend the rest of your life in jail?

It's obviously a good rule, wherever it came from. You can stop holding your breath, granny—he's not going to.

All right, I admit that's a pretty facetious example. But that's the way I want you to tackle it. That's the way I want you to break it down and analyse it. Think about the road to personal success that's opening up before you as you read this book. See if you can find out what rules are likely to stand in your way.

You're a married man with kids. Every weekend you take the kids out into the country, because you figure that's good for them, you figure a man should have time for his children. You do it every weekend, so whether you realized it or not, that's one of your rules. Where did it come from? You think back and find that, seven years ago, you read something in a book by a psychologist that said it was good for a businessman to have time for his children.

Seems like a good rule really. *But keep digging!* Every rule you have will seem like a good rule to begin with. That's why you've never questioned them before. Did the psychologist know what he was talking about? Just because something's written down in a book doesn't mean it's true (not even when it's written down in *this* book). What's the psychologist's reputation? Was the rest of his advice sound? And hey—maybe your kids don't like the country. Maybe they'd be happier playing with their friends instead of tramping round with an old goat like you. Or maybe they used to like the country seven years ago, when you read the book, but they've gone off it now (who wouldn't, having been dragged out every weekend for seven years?). Maybe psychological opinion has changed in the last seven years. Maybe the up-to-date opinion is that only a lunatic drags his children off to the country. Maybe your children would be better off if you worked weekends and brought in some extra money. . . .

See what I mean? Even when you have what looks like a cast iron good rule it only looks really good while it's unconscious. Once you take it out in the open and examine it, all sorts of things start to emerge.

It may well be that when you've examined it, you'll decide the rule really is a good one, well worth keeping. That's great. Just so long as you've pulled it out in the open and made a conscious reasonable decision. But if you find the rule doesn't stand up to the light of day, throw it out fast. There's no way you need to be weighed down by a load of useless rules. And you'd be amazed how useless some rules are. One patient of mine never asked out good-looking women. Never. At parties and dances, he'd take home plain girls. The good-lookers he'd leave on the shelf. That was one of his rules. It came from his mother, who was a plain woman and who told him when he was small that good-looking women were gold-diggers. So he made that a rule. Once he had it out in the open, he could see how silly it was. He's engaged to a good-looking woman now, and I know she's going to make him a fine wife.

So look at all your rules—your work patterns, your emotional patterns, your lifestyle, your prejudices. Find out the rules you're living by. Figure out where they came from. Then see how sound they are. And if they aren't sound, if you can't find good, conscious, logical reasons for them . . . ditch them.

You can start doing all that, right now, in your armchair. When you think you've examined every rule you have, take a break, then start again. Believe me, there's a lot of work involved. And while you can start it in your armchair, you're going to have to keep it up in the process of day-to-day living.

Maybe it's not such a lazy man's step after all.

When you've thrown out as much of the clutter as you can manage, come back to this book. Because the process of change is only beginning. But the next thing you're going to learn really *is* lazy. And very nice.

*   *   *

Before you make the changes in your mind that will help turn you into a success person, you're going to have to make a few changes in your body. No, I'm not about to advocate jogging, weight-lifting or the latest executive fad diet. You can play around with all those things if you like. But they aren't going to do a bit of good until you learn how to relax.

Relaxation

Relaxation's a grand thing, even in isolation. It can stop you getting wrinkles or a heart attack. It can help you conserve precious energy for the times when you really need it. It can wipe out symptoms you might have mistaken for a full-blown neurosis if you didn't know better. But within the confines of the present book, I'm not suggesting you should learn to relax for any of these reasons, excellent though they might be. I want you to learn to relax so you can start those mental disciplines which are going to change your negative self-image and wipe out a good few of those imaginary limitations. Because until you learn to relax, the mental disciplines won't work.

Relaxation sounds like it's the easiest thing in the world. All you do is stop working, sit down and do it. Easy. But it's not. In our culture, relaxation is just about the hardest thing in the world. People used to pay me big chunks of their hard-earned money just to show them how to do it. That's really amazing when you think about it: intelligent human beings paying out good money to learn how to do something a cat does naturally eighty per cent of its time.

There are a lot of funny ideas floating round about relaxation; and about the opposite side of the coin, tension. A feeling of relaxation is very pleasant to experience. A feeling of tension isn't. This has led a lot of people to believe tension is somehow wrong. This is a fallacy. Tension is only wrong when it's inappropriate to the situation.

Let me explain with an outlandish example. Suppose you were strolling through the park one day when you turned a corner and came face to face with an insane man-eating lion which had escaped from the zoo and missed three meal times. Would you get tense? Damn right you'd get tense! There'd be something badly wrong with you if you didn't. Furthermore, tension would be the best possible thing for you to feel in the circumstances. When you're faced with a man-eating lion, the thing to do is get out of there fast. Your muscles need to be tight, your adrenalin pumping, your heart racing and your mind clear. All keyed to getting your legs moving faster than they've ever moved before. Stand there and relax, and the next thing you know the lion's chewing off your arm. As an *hors d'oeuvre*.

There is tension *appropriate to the situation*. But the situation doesn't have to be anything as crazy as lions in the park. It could be a tough Board meeting. Or a big sales conference. Or a confrontation with the boss about how badly he's been paying you. When you hit the success circuit, you're going to experience dozens of situations where tension is appropriate. It keys you up to do your very best.

Unfortunately, another of the nasty tricks Nature plays on the human race is something called *conditioning*. A Russian psychologist called Pavlov discovered the mechanics of conditioning quite a few years ago. He set up a series of experiments involving dogs. What he did, basically, was this:

Every time Pavlov fed his dogs, he noticed they salivated. That is, their mouths watered at the sight of food. That's normal enough, and since the dogs can't control the action, it's called a reflex. During the series of experiments, Pavlov decided to ring a bell every time he presented food. So you had a sequence: bell . . . food . . . mouth watering. He did this dozens of times. Then one day he rang the bell, but didn't produce food. The mouth-watering reflex still came up. Pavlov concluded the reflex had become conditional on the bell rather than the food. A slight error in translation has led us to call this conditioned reflex. The process of artificially tying reflex actions to some controllable outside stimulus, is now called conditioning.

When you meet your lion in the park, the tension you feel is a reflex. It's right outside your conscious control. And at first, the reflex is conditional on the lion, as it should be. But if you keep on meeting lions in the park, pretty soon you're going to build up a conditioned tension reflex that's associated with the park rather than the lion. Given time—and not all that much time, either—you're going to get tense every time you walk into that park, whether you meet a lion or not.

We've already said that the lion in the park is an outlandish example of the process. But the process is there, ready to work at any time. You may not meet lions, but you certainly meet dozens of naturally tension-producing situations. The result is that you get conditioned to tension.

But doesn't this mean just about everybody gets conditioned to tension? Yes, it does. It may sound as outlandish as lions in the park, but let me assure you just about everybody suffers from tension to some degree or other. And the reason they suffer is conditioning.

Tension Habits

Another word for conditioning is habit. Over a lifetime you build up tension habits. Everybody builds up tension habits. And I mean *everybody*. Even the man who thinks he's perfectly relaxed. Even the man who *looks* as if he's perfectly relaxed.

The trouble with tension is that it's largely unconscious. People get tense (and stay tense) without for a moment realizing what's happened to them. They go through life thinking they're pretty much relaxed, but all the time they're suffering from tension at an unconscious level. And that's why relaxation's so difficult. That's why people used to pay me good money to teach them how to do it. They couldn't tackle the job themselves, because they didn't know where tension lay.

By now you must be wondering how true all this is. You probably feel very much relaxed right now, reading this book and thinking ahead to the days when you'll be enjoying the fruits of personal success. You probably think the people around you are pretty much relaxed too. So what's all this talk about everybody suffering from tension?

All right, I'll prove it to you. You're going to need a partner for this experiment. Except that it isn't just an experiment. It's the first step towards achieving relaxation. When you've found a willing partner, decide whether he's going to be the guinea pig (in which case you'll prove he's not totally relaxed) or whether you're going to be the guinea pig (in which case he'll prove it's you who's suffering from tension). It doesn't matter which way you do it. But for the sake of clarity, I'm going to assume you're the doctor and he's the patient.

Have your friend lie down flat on his back, on a bed or on the floor. If you're using a bed, take away the pillow: he needs to be completely flat to begin with. Make sure he doesn't cross his legs or clasp his hands. The arms should be lying straight out along the sides of his body. Now invite him to relax as completely as he's able. Tell him to let you know when he's totally relaxed. When he tells you, ask him to stay that way. Tell him you're going to test him for relaxation. Tell him he's not to try to help you in anything you do. All he has to do is stay relaxed.

Right. Now slide your hand underneath the ankle of the right leg and lift. If he's relaxed, the leg will feel heavy. When you let go, it will fall back down with a thud. If he's not relaxed, the leg will feel light—and may even stay up there after you let go.

Repeat this process with the left leg, then with each arm in turn. Then move on to his head. Unless your friend is very tense indeed, you should have found positive relaxation reactions on both arms and legs. But when you come to lift his head up, you will almost certainly find he tries to help. He will raise it a little for you to allow you to get your hands underneath. This is the first sign of tension. Tell him gently not to help, just to leave his neck relaxed and try again. Some people find it so difficult to relax the neck muscles that they will continue to lift the head even after you've reminded them not to help. Keep gently reminding them until they get the hang of it.

Lift the head only an inch or two, then let it drop. If he's relaxed, it will come down with a thud. (That's why you only lift it an inch or two — it's difficult to relax somebody with a cracked skull). Now move on to the shoulders, one at a time. You'll almost certainly find tension here too.

If I'm right so far, you've already proved your friend isn't nearly so relaxed as he thought he was. But there may be a lot more tension in there yet. Roll is head gently to the left and to the right. If he's relaxed, it really will roll. If he's tense, it won't.

Now comes something really dramatic — something people don't usually believe until they see it with their own eyes. Go back to his right leg. Slip your right hand under the ankle as before, and your left hand under the back of the thigh, just above the knee joint. Lift the whole leg, using both hands, and let it drop. By now he'll be getting the hang of the process and the leg will probably drop heavily. Repeat the movement, only this time, instead of letting go with both hands, *only let go with your right hand*. This means you're still supporting the top of the leg with your left hand under the back of the thigh. If your friend's leg is relaxed, the leg will bend at the knee. The bottom part of the leg and foot will drop, leaving you supporting the remainder with your left hand. But chances are this won't happen. Chances are that leg will stay straight as a ramrod, pointing right up at an angle of 45 degrees. I've had patients who were so tense I couldn't get the knee to bend even when I pushed hard down on the ankle. Yet they still swore the leg was relaxed.

The funny thing is that, even when you've shown a really tense person where their tension lies, they still find it difficult to let go. You can point out there's tension in the right leg, have them relax it so it bends at the knee, then do the same thing with the left leg and they'll still hold it rigid when you let go with one hand.

When you've finished with the legs, move on finally to the stomach. Place one hand, palm down, on his stomach just about the navel. Place your other hand on top, then press down gently. Since all a human being's important organs are inside there, you'll find in most cases there's an automatic protection response. The stomach muscles tighten. Point this out to him and see if you can persuade him to relax them.

By the time you've gone through this whole process—or somebody else has gone through it on you—you'll have proved your friend is carrying round a lot more tension than he thought. Throughout my entire clinical practice, when I used this technique on more people than I can remember, only one showed himself capable of relaxing completely. He was an American, and when he let himself go, he was *really* able to let himself go. He relaxed so well, I was astonished. I simply didn't believe anybody could relax that well without help. But then it turned out he was a yoga practitioner. He'd been practising relaxation and meditation daily for years. No wonder he was able to relax completely.

Which brings me to my next important point. If you're going to learn how to relax, you have to work at it. You have to work at it daily and have to work at it for quite a long time. Just as you unconsciously built up a tension habit, so you have consciously to build up a relaxation habit.

The key word there is 'consciously'. That's why I said the test procedure was the first step towards learning how to relax. Because the test procedure makes you conscious of where your tension centres are.

In the next chapter, you'll find out how to put this knowledge to use.

5

Total Relaxation

Here's a strange thing. The first secret of relaxing your muscles has nothing to do with relaxing your muscles. It has to do with breathing.

Everybody breathes. It's the very first priority of your life, every moment of every day of your life. But not everybody breathes correctly.

Assume we're carrying on where we left off. You've just shown your friend the truth about his tension centres. He's still lying there on his back, amazed to find how tense he was, and wondering if the world will ever be the same again. Put your hands back on his stomach, exactly as before. But this time press down firmly, and keep pressing down. (So long as you don't do it suddenly it won't hurt. If it does hurt, stop pressing instantly—he may have an ulcer or some other internal trouble). Now, while you're pressing down, invite him to breathe in deeply. Watch what happens.

As your friend breathes in deeply, his chest will rise. Now move your hands up and place them on the bottom of his chest, near where the rib-cage ends. Once again press down firmly, hold it and invite him to breathe deeply. This time, his stomach will rise.

His stomach will rise because the air he's breathing in has to go somewhere. In the first case, it went into the top of his lungs, and this expanded his chest. In the second case, you were pressing down on the chest so it couldn't expand to the same degree. As a result, the air went on down to the bottom of his lungs, and that meant stomach expansion.

Military men like to see troops walking around with their chests expanded like pouter pigeons and their stomachs pulled well in. Which may be a good way to fight a war (although that's a debatable point), but it's not a good way to breathe. Because breathing with the top of your lungs limits your intake of oxygen. And that in turn limits your powers of relaxation (it's also bad for you in a lot of other ways, but that's beside the point here). So from now on, whenever you breathe, I want you to make a habit of breathing with your stomach. If your stomach isn't moving when you breathe, you're doing it wrong. Until you get the hang of it, there'll be lots of times when you forget. Don't worry about that—just keep trying. But never forget to breathe with your stomach when you're doing a relaxation exercise. It doesn't have to be big deep breaths. It doesn't have to be a strain. Just so long as you're breathing with your stomach.

The benefit of the business with your friend was that it shows you where your tensions lie, brings them up to consciousness. The benefit of breathing with your stomach is that it fills your lungs properly and allows better oxygenation of the bloodstream. Which feeds the muscles properly. And muscles are like the people who own them: they tend to relax better after a good meal.

Building up a Relaxation Habit

The benefit of the next exercise I'm going to teach you incorporates a bit of both these approaches. It allows you to get a conscious grip on tension, and at the same time starts you building up a habit of relaxation. This exercise is so simple you might be tempted to undervalue it. Don't. It's a magnificent way of achieving total relaxation. And it's so easy that you can do it (or at least do modified versions of it) almost anywhere and almost anytime. I've used it a lot in the past to relax people prior to inducing an hypnotic trance. Doctor friends tell me it's one of the standard pre-natal exercises given to pregnant women, so they can relax during childbirth.

I'd like you to try to do this exercise fully at least once a day for two and a half to three months. Starting today. This may seem to you like a long time, but what we're trying to do here is build up a relaxation habit. We're building in a conditioned reflex of relaxation. You've had years for the tension habit to build up, so a few months isn't all that long to devote to relaxation. Besides which, though it takes a bit of time to describe, the exercise itself takes very little time to do—less than five minutes. And if you can find time to manage it twice a day, you'll be totally relaxed all that much sooner.

Here's what you do:

Lie down on your back, arms by your side, feet uncrossed. Make yourself comfortable in this position. Take off your shoes if they're tight. Loosen your tie. Wriggle around and make yourself comfortable. Remember, you should be breathing with your stomach.

Now curl your toes and feet downwards, away from your body. This will create a considerable amount of tension in your feet. Press hard so it's really uncomfortable. Think about the feeling of tension in your feet. Think hard. I want you to know what tension feels like. And I want you to know it from conscious, considered experience.

Now let go. Feel the discomfort ease. Feel your feet uncurl. Feel the muscles relax. Take time to think about the difference between the feeling of tension and the feeling of relaxation.

Now move on to the next set of muscles, which is the calf muscles. You can tighten them by moving your feet the other way, so your toes point back up towards your body. Once again hold it, thinking about tension. Then let go. Then think about the difference between the feeling of tension and the feeling of relaxation.

Got the sequence? Tension . . . thought . . . relaxation . . . thought. Still breathing with your stomach? Fine.

On now to your thigh muscles. Do exactly the same here. Tighten them as tight as they'll go. Think about the tension. Then let them go loose and think about the difference between what you were feeling then and what you are feeling now.

Try your hands next, tightening them into fists.

Next your stomach, pulling it in really tight, holding it tight, then relaxing as before.

Next shoulders. This tends to be a big tension centre—all those muscles at the base of the neck. It's worth taking a bit of extra time here, hunching your shoulders tight, thinking about what you're feeling, then relaxing and noticing the difference.

Now on to the face. You have an awful lot of little muscles in the face and worried people keep them tense almost all the time (you use more muscles to frown than you do to smile, which must mean something). Make a face, screw up your eyes. Grit your teeth tightly. I know you'll feel a bit silly, but that doesn't matter. Hold everything tight, think about it, then let go.

And finally, your scalp. Frown to bring the scalp forward. Some people can't do this at all. If you're one of them, don't worry—the scalp muscles are one of those sets of muscles which are deteriorating in the course of our evolutionary development, because we don't need to use them much. But if yours are still working, tense them, think about it, then relax.

At this stage you have consciously tensed and relaxed every major set of muscles in your body—including those that tend to be a particular prey to tension. Now let's see if we can get you even more relaxed. Go over those various sets of muscles in your mind. If you find tension has crept back in again to any of them, tighten it up further, then consciously let go. When you've done this, tighten up every muscle in your body—every one. Hold yourself absolutely rigid, tight and tense. Think about the feeling of extreme physical tension. Hold it. Then let go. Think about the difference. Now sigh deeply, aloud.

Feeling better? I thought you might be. It's a very simple exercise, but one that's highly effective. Use it at least once every day from now on—twice a day or more if you can manage. You're building up a relaxation habit—and that's important work. It will help you feel better, live longer and it will lay the foundations of personal success. So don't put the exercise aside because you're 'too busy' or 'too tired'. There are very few things you could be doing that are more important than building up a relaxation habit.

Now I've got bad news and good news.

The bad news is that even after doing that exercise, you're still not totally relaxed. Oh, you may feel pretty relaxed. And you *are* more relaxed than you were to begin with. But you're still not totally relaxed.

The good news is that you can soon learn how to achieve total relaxation.

*   *   *

So far, we've been dealing exclusively with your body. But, as you may have noticed, your body isn't all there is to you. If you think back to our example of lions in the park and what we said about conditioning, you'll quickly realize that the ultimate root of tension isn't in the body at all (except in rare cases of disease). The ultimate root of tension is in the mind.

Right now we're going to get together to tackle tension at a mental level. By this I don't mean we're going to wipe out your worries. That's something which will come later. I mean instead that we're going to use mental techniques to increase your level of physical relaxation.

The techniques we're going to use are connected with imagination and visualization. I've already said imagination is an underrated business. Now I'd like to go on record telling you how underrated I think it is.

IMAGINATION IS THE MOST IMPORTANT TECHNIQUE IN YOUR PURSUIT OF PERSONAL SUCCESS.

That's how underrated I think it is. When you use your imagination, when you visualize to yourself, most people tell you you're 'only daydreaming'. Most people think you're swinging the lead, engaged in the most useless, futile occupation you could possibly find.

But they're wrong. And a minute's thought will convince you how wrong they are. If you worry yourself into an ulcer or a heart attack imagining the bad things that might happen tomorrow, you have to admit at least that imagination's very strong medicine. So strong it can savage your body, or kill you. And if you start to think about the great symphonies,

the great paintings, the great novels, plays and artworks—
they all started out as acts of imagination. Before they were
composed, painted, written, they all existed in the world of
the imagination. While you're at it, you could do worse than
thinking about the great engineering works, the great
inventions, the physical techniques we use to control our
environment, make things comfortable. Every last one of
them started out as an idea in somebody's imagination.
That's how powerful imagination can be.

As you continue to read this book, you'll learn ways of
putting this enormous power to work for you. With results
outside your wildest dreams. I'll start by showing you a
simple—but important—use of imagination. That way
you'll experience the power at first hand. Starting right now,
you're going to learn how to use imagination to achieve total
relaxation.

I'm assuming you've just finished the physical relaxation
exercise just described. You've given a big, deep sigh and
you're lying on your back feeling pretty good, pretty relaxed.
Now start to imagine that something's happening to your
muscles. It's something very odd. Every muscle in your body
is growing longer. It's growing long and limp. Lie there and
visualize this strongly. See the muscles getting longer and
longer and drooping. Keep at it until you're imagining so
strongly that your muscles actually begin to feel that way.
Long and limp. Long and limp. Repeat those words to
yourself, over and over, in your mind. Long and limp.

Notice the difference it's making to your degree of
relaxation?

Here's another exercise:

Lie there and imagine you're growing heavy. Imagine
you've just been given an injection in the foot that slowly
turns every cell in your body to an atom of lead.

Lie there and imagine how heavy your feet are growing.
They're turning to lead. And the process is creeping up your
body, along your legs, into your trunk and arms . . . every
muscle and fibre slowly turning to lead. Imagine this
strongly. Feel the pressure of your body on the bed. Feel how
heavy you've grown. Imagine the bed creaking and groaning
under your weight. Now your neck has turned to lead. Your

head has turned to lead. You now weigh several tons. It's amazing you don't break right through the bed: maybe it was better built than you thought. You're so heavy now, it's a real effort to move even a finger.

Notice the difference it's making to your degree of relaxation?

Here's another:

Imagine you can actually see your blood flow. Imagine your skin has suddenly turned transparent and you can see the flow of blood in the body, warm and cosy, bathing the muscles with relaxing balm. Imagine the warmth creeping up from your feet. Feel how comfortably warm your body is getting. Warmth in your legs, your abdomen, your chest. Warmth in your face. Feel the flow of lovely warmth moving down your back. And once again, notice the difference it makes to your degree of relaxation.

Give another deep sigh, out loud, and try this next imagination exercise—the simplest of the lot.

Imagine you've suddenly become a rag doll. You know those rag dolls little girls play with—the ones they drag about by the leg. A floppy, bendy, rag doll that just collapses when you drop it. A rag doll that straggles all over the place when you throw it down. That's what you are now, arms and legs thrown out, limp and floppy. See your rag-doll muscles. They're made from wool! Limp, floppy wool. It's a ridiculous thought, but stay with it. Visualize the muscles individually and see them in your mind's eye, drooping down there like a handful of wool. Here again you'll find a difference to your degree of relaxation.

You'll probably find that one of these imagination exercises works better for you than the others. Maybe it just appeals to you more. Maybe you find it just that little bit easier to visualize.

That's the exercise I want you to use from now on—the one that suits you best. I want you to use it every day, immediately after you've finished the physical relaxation exercise. I want you to work on that visualization until it becomes as real to you as the room around you. And if you get tense during the day—at any time during the day—I want you to use the exercise again to help you relax. Keep using your favourite visualization after the physical relaxation exercise, keep doing it day after day (even Saturdays and Sundays), keep at it faithfully and consistently, and I'll guarantee the day will come when you've achieved total relaxation. When that day comes, you can start relaxing your way to personal success.

Which is what we'll be discussing in the next chapter.

6

Relaxing Your Way To Success

In business, there are a lot of benefits to relaxation.

For a start, people relate to you better. You can see this for yourself, any day of the week, just by watching the reverse — which is, unfortunately, more commonplace. Any salesman who's uptight and tense when he approaches you won't sell you a thing. He won't sell you a scrambled egg if you're starving. He won't sell you a new, guaranteed Rolls Royce for a fiver. Because all the time you're wondering what's wrong, where the catch is. All the time, you're feeling uncomfortable.

The reason you're feeling uncomfortable is because nervousness is infectious. You can see that any day of the week, too. Place one really uptight person in a nice, relaxed gathering and if you're not careful, more and more people suddenly start getting uptight too. Before you know it, the gathering is a nervous wreck.

Maybe that's a slight exaggeration, but not much. Translate the example into a business environment, and you can see why tension is such bad news on the road to personal success. People don't like you as well, when you're tense. You make them feel uncomfortable. And as long as they feel uncomfortable, they aren't about to do you any business favours.

Furthermore, you don't work at your best when you're tense. I'm not talking about appropriate tension, of course.

That's the kind that keys you up to the job on hand. I'm talking about inappropriate, conditioned, habit tension, which actually drains away your energy, leaves you washed out and feeble, keeps your mind circulating round your worries instead of around the job at hand. That sort of tension makes you work at a fraction of your potential all the time. Pretty soon, people start to notice. And suddenly your road to personal success has turned into a cul-de-sac.

Confidence and Competence Go Together

Now, relaxation—the total, habitual relaxation you'll build up with the exercises in the last chapter—works just the opposite way. People enjoy relaxed company. It makes them feel comfortable and well-disposed towards you. More important still, a relaxed man positively exudes confidence. And confident (or apparently confident) people get more of the breaks. Confidence and competence go hand in hand. If you exude confidence, people trust you. If you exude confidence, you'll be given more important jobs to do.

While we're on the point, I might as well mention there are two types of confidence. One is tense confidence, which comes across as pushy and cocky. The other is relaxed confidence, which comes across as competence. I don't need to tell you which is likely to be the more successful.

But relaxation is important to you for another reason. Once you learn how to relax totally, you can start making changes in that negative self-image we talked about. You can also do something about your imaginary limitations. Remember the hint I gave at the end of the first chapter? Since imagination put your limitations up there in the first place, imagination is the thing to use to take them down again.

You've already seen how imagination can help you control your muscles, can help you achieve total relaxation. Believe me, that's not all it can do, not by a long chalk. Imagination can help you change your *attitudes*. It can also—although you're going to find this harder to believe—change your circumstances.

Since I don't know you personally, I don't know exactly what changes you need to make. So I can't write down a series of imagination exercises and promise you success if you take the course. But I can show you the type of imagination exercise you should be doing. And I can give you some general exercises which will help you along the way. The only thing you have to remember is that these exercises aren't the secret formula of success. You'll have to modify them to suit your own personality and circumstances.

But once you make the modifications in accordance with the rules I'll give, you will have the secret formula of success. And it will be your own personal secret formula.

*   *   *

Emil Coué was an exponent of the art of auto-suggestion. His phrase, 'Every day, in every way, I am getting better and better', became world famous in his time and is still quoted to the present day. Coué, a dapper little Frenchman, was enormously successful for a time and his system enjoyed an international vogue. But it eventually transpired that it was not the miracle it had seemed at first. For while some of Coué's followers did indeed get better and better, many didn't. One problem was that, while Coué told people what to say to themselves, he didn't tell them when to say it. Or how. With those two missing keys, auto-suggestion can be a very potent system indeed. One that can literally change your life.

Self-suggestion works best when you are totally relaxed. It doesn't work at all when you are tense. That's one thing many of Coué's followers missed.

Let's not make an old mistake twice. Before you start to tackle your negative self-image, your imaginary limitations, make sure you're totally relaxed. You can achieve that by practising the relaxation exercises I've already described. Once you can become totally relaxed at will, you can tackle negative self-image and imagination limitations any time, as often as necessary. But until that day comes, you can still do some good twice a day. There are two times in every day when you are naturally totally relaxed. Those times are:

1. First thing in the morning, immediately after waking up.
2. Last thing at night, immediately before falling asleep.

Neither time lasts very long. After a few minutes in the

morning, the worries of the day start crowding in on you and the old tension habits take over. At night you finally fall asleep—and if you think sleep's a relaxing time, you've never watched the typical threshing around of a sleeper.

But before the worries start and before sleep claims you, you go through a brief spell scientists have called the 'hypnogogic period'. It's the nice, dreamy stage before you're properly asleep, when you're not quite awake either. All sorts of peculiar things happen in the hypnogogic period. Some people hear voices. Some get snatches of visions. But everybody is totally relaxed, and capable, with a bit of willpower, of mental action.

The mental action I want you to take is a form of self-suggestion, which brings me to the second weakness in Coué's system. Coué maintained you should couch your self-suggestion in words. Like, 'Every day and in every way. . . .' The trouble is, words don't always work.

Let me take up a minute of your time with a little lecture on how your mind works. First off, as you know, your mind is divided into two areas: the conscious and the unconscious. In your normal waking state, some sort of barrier exists between your conscious and your unconscious mind. This is no bad thing, because it prevents unconscious elements erupting into consciousness with such force that you walk under a 'bus. The barrier is not absolutely rigid, for you know *some* unconscious contents do get through—which is why you sometimes have strange feelings, irrational depressions, intuitions, compulsions and the rest. But by and large, the barrier does a pretty good job. It seems to work even better in reverse. When it's up, your conscious mind has a very difficult time getting through to your unconscious.

Contacting Your Subconscious

When you relax, however, the barrier lowers. This seems to happen automatically. It explains why some people hear voices and see visions in the hypnogogic period. It explains why we dream when we're asleep. The more deeply you relax, the more the barrier lowers. This means that when you're relaxed, there's a greater chance of your conscious mind getting messages through to your unconscious. When you're totally relaxed, this message-passing potential is at a peak. But even a direct line to China won't do you much good if you can't speak Chinese. And it's equally pointless talking to your unconscious mind if you're using language it doesn't understand.

Now, the unconscious mind is a lot older than the conscious. That's true in both evolutionary and individual terms. As a baby, your unconscious mind was working full steam long before you were able to think consciously. As an evolutionary fact, the unconscious was developed over millions of years before the first glimmer of consciousness appeared on the scene. The age difference between your conscious and your unconscious will give you the clue to the sort of 'language' the unconscious uses. It's basically a primitive construction, a type of sign language. For while your conscious mind thinks in *words*, your unconscious mind thinks in *pictures*. Until you start to talk in pictures, you're not talking the language the unconscious easily understands.

Coué's auto-suggestions were framed in words, so they were difficult for the unconscious to understand. *Your* self-suggestions should be presented in pictorial form. That way, they have a far better chance of working as you want them to. By all this, I simply mean that when you begin to tackle your negative self-image, your imaginary limitations, you should do so not by mentally telling yourself things, but by mentally showing yourself pictures.

Okay, let's get down to basics. From now on, each night and morning when you're in the hypnogogic period, I want you to visualize certain things. In every case, I want you to visualize as clearly as possible. And in every case, I want you to visualize in as much detail as possible. Detail is very important. One clear, detailed picture is worth a dozen hazy daydreams. In fact, detail is so very important that I'll be spelling out exactly what I mean in a moment.

Don't feel you have to hold these visualizations for a long time. You don't; and in any case, you can't at this stage, because the hypnogogic state lasts only a short time. Later, when you can totally relax at will, you may like to devote a little more time to your visualization programme. But the important thing is *regularity*. Three minutes . . . two minutes

. . . even one minute visualization *every* day is worth far more than several hours done together once a week.

Visualization Techniques

So, what do you have to visualize? One fine way of hitting out at both your negative self-image and your imaginary limitations is to visualize yourself. But visualize yourself *not as you are, but as you wish to be*. That's the crucial difference. That's the dagger that stabs your negative self-image to death, that hacks away your imaginary limitations. All through your life you've visualized yourself in a negative way. This is literally true, because we've already seen how your negative self-image was built up in the unconscious, and we know the unconscious thinks in pictures. So every time your unconscious mind thought about you, it built up a negative picture. Every time you wanted to do something, your unconscious checked your capacity to do it against that negative picture, and very often that unconscious yardstick found you wanting.

But once you visualize yourself not as you are, but as you wish to be, you're firmly telling your unconscious that things have changed. You're telling your unconscious you're no longer a weak, helpless child, but an intelligent, active, powerful adult.

There's a very subtle point hidden here. I've instructed you to visualize yourself not as you are. At the same time, I've gone to great pains earlier to suggest you really are a lot better than you think. But no matter how often I tell you, you're not going to believe me until your negative self-image has changed. So if you were to try to visualize yourself as you are, you'd never manage it. Instead, you'd visualize yourself as you thought you were. And that would defeat the whole purpose of the exercise.

It's a little like judo, which uses subtlety and skill instead of strength. Let's accept for the moment that you're weak and limited (it's not true, but let's accept it anyway). Let's accept it . . . and forget about it, because it's just that image we're setting out to change. In your visualizations, see yourself *as you wish to be*. And as you visualize, don't make the mistake of limiting yourself again. If you find this difficult, remember you're working in the realm of the imagination. And in this realm, anything is possible.

As I said earlier, I can't tell you exactly what to visualize, because I don't know you personally, so I don't know what you want to be. But I'd like to give you a few examples of the type of thing you might be visualizing. Which certainly isn't to say this is what you should be visualizing—because only you know that.

Let's suppose one of your big hang-ups is your appearance. Let's be blunt and suppose you think you're fat. Let's be even blunter and assume you really *are* fat. Being overweight is no joke. It can sap your energy, ruin the way clothes look on you, inhibit your sexual magnetism and generally grow up into a pretty serious problem. So you're fat and you want to be thin. Or do you? The chances are you don't want to be thin as much as slim. Even if you aren't happy being overweight, you wouldn't be all that happy as a walking beanpole either. This is what I was getting at earlier when I said you have to visualize in detail.

The only way you're going to build up a proper visualization is to work out, in advance, exactly how you want to look. And I mean *exactly*. Let's suppose you now weigh 13 stone (182 lbs) and you figure this is grossly overweight. Ask yourself *how much* overweight it is. A stone? Two stone? A stone and a half? If you decide, for example, you are two stone (28 lbs) overweight, then first visualize yourself standing on a weighing scale. See the pointer on that scale in your mind's eye. And see it pointing firmly to 11 stone (154 lbs). That's what I mean by detail. If you're visualizing properly, you should even be able to read the manufacturer's name on the scales!

Now see yourself as you want to look. Losing a couple of stone is fine, but if the weight doesn't come off the right places, it still isn't going to improve your appearance all that much. So now visualize yourself stepping off the scales and going to look at yourself in a full-length bathroom mirror. Visualize yourself naked (in your imagination, no-one's likely to be looking). And visualize yourself as you wish to be. See that flat stomach. See that well-developed chest. See the muscle tone. See the clear skin. See the healthy shine in your hair. See the strong, straight legs. If you fancy hair on your chest (and haven't got any in reality), see hair on your chest—as much or as little as you want. If you're having trouble with early baldness, visualize fresh hair growth on your head. It doesn't matter if your doctor's told you fresh hair growth is impossible: visualize it anyway.

In this exercise, as in all visualization exercises, the basic rule is that you must not limit yourself in any way. So if you feel you'd look better with subtle changes in your features, go ahead and visualize that too. And visualize in detail. You're standing in front of a bathroom mirror. You should be able to see the colour of the wall behind it. You should be able to feel the texture of the carpet beneath your bare feet. You should be able to smell the soap on the washbasin behind you. That's *detailed* visualization. Even incidental details are important, because the picture has to convince your unconscious mind.

Works Like 'Magic'

Let me tell you something spooky. Once you start doing a visualization like this properly, you really will start to lose weight. And you'll start to lose it off the right places. I've watched this happen to dozens of my clients. It happened fast when they went on a diet, but it still happened slowly even if they didn't. Sounds like magic, but it isn't. Your unconscious is that part of your mind which controls most of your body processes—your heartbeat, your blood pressure, your pain threshold, your metabolism and so on. Once you get your unconscious working through you, it can control a lot of things your conscious can't. Like your appetitie, or the workings of your thyroid gland. As a result, your unconscious can make those fine metabolic adjustments which lead to your becoming slim. It can make them so subtly that you never even notice. So total relaxation, combined with visualization, means you really can 'think yourself thin'.

What else can you do?

I picked the fat-to-thin example for a reason: the results are clear-cut and indisputable. You move from 13 stone to 11 stone. The difference can be measured. The weight loss can be read off on a scale. When it happens, there's no doubt at all about what this visualization did. But chances are weight isn't one of your hang-ups. It may be you're troubled by something a lot more subtle, like lack of confidence. If that's the pattern you want to change, you might tackle it this way:

1. Decide in advance the sort of confidence you want to project. Quietly confident. Aggressively confident. Super-confident. Relaxed and confident. Enthusiastic and confident. Or whatever. Make this decision carefully and consciously, in advance.

2. During your hypnogogic period, visualize yourself not with the level of confidence you have now, but with the level and type you wish to project. This can't be as straight-forward as visualizing yourself looking in the bathroom mirror, because confidence doesn't show as plainly as slimmness does. In fact, confidence doesn't show at all in a solitary situation, so this visualization will have to take account of the circumstances in which you want to feel confident.

Once again, I can only guess at what those circumstances might be in your individual case. Maybe you're like a client of mine, a university lecturer who wanted to increase his confidence when he appeared on a public platform before an audience of people. Maybe you're like another client of mine who just wanted to feel confident when he walked in to his boss's office to ask for a rise. Or maybe you want to feel more confident socially—at dinner parties, cocktail parties and so on. Maybe you must want to feel more confident with the opposite sex. The possibilities are almost endless.

Let's take one or two at random and see what sort of visualization fits the bill. We'll start with a difficult one. You want to feel more confident at parties.

First off, figure out how you behave at parties at the moment. Could be you're happy enough when you know everybody there, and it's only a party full of strangers which makes you feel uncomfortable. Or maybe you're okay at stag (or hen) parties and it's only a mixed social gathering which triggers your inferiority complex. Think about what you do now in such situations. You may drink too much. Or sit in a corner. Or closet yourself with one sympathetic soul and refuse to mix.

Now start your visualization. Build up in your mind's eye the type of party you absolutely hate. The one that makes you feel the most uncomfortable. Build it up carefully and in detail. See the faces of the people, the dresses of the women, the colour of the carpet and the walls. Hear the music playing in the background. Notice what sort of drinks are being served. Listen to the conversation that's going on. Make this as clear and real and detailed as you're able.

When you've done all that, visualize yourself at that party, not as you are, but as you wish to be. See yourself calm and confident. Picture yourself clearly, so that if someone asked you what was in the glass in your hand, you could tell them instantly. Know what you're wearing. See yourself enjoying yourself. Circulating for a change. Entertaining people with your conversation. Charming members of the opposite sex. Intriguing the wise and powerful with your wit. Above all, visualize the reactions of other people to you. Visualize warm, positive reactions to everything you say and do. Know that at this party, you're well-liked and popular.

That's a difficult one, as I said. There's a lot of detail to visualize. Let's try another example that's simpler. Let's suppose you want confidence to go in and ask your boss for a rise.

Once again, you should do a little prior preparation. It's pointless starting on this visualization until you know how much extra money you want. Exactly. To the penny. Decide in advance whether it's another five, ten, fifteen or fifty pounds a week you need. Decide why you're worth it. Have your arguments ready in advance. Now visualize your boss's office. That should be fairly easy since you've probably been in there quite often. Visualize in detail. Visualize your boss himself. But make sure to visualize him in a good mood. Assume he's really happy because he's just pulled off a big business deal. Things are going really well for him. He's feeling benevolent and loves the world. Especially, he loves *you*. Now visualize yourself going in there confidently and asking for the rise. Asking for exactly the amount of extra money you decided in advance. And—this is important—visualize yourself getting it. See your boss smiling and nodding and agreeing with every point you make. See him shaking your hand, hear him congratulating you on the quality of your work to date. Finally, see yourself examining your paypacket, or your monthly cheque. Notice that the extra money has been included.

Once again you're hoisting up a signal to your own unconscious mind, showing it what you want, persuading it to work for you instead of against you. It still isn't magic, but the results will seem like magic when they happen.

These are just a few examples of the type of visualization you might undertake. It's up to you to decide exactly what it is you need to visualize. When you've decided, go to it. But remember, visualization is useless until you're totally relaxed or in the hypnogogic period. And fuzzy visualization is almost as bad as no visualization at all, so make it *detailed*.

Finally, give your visualizations time. You're not going to do the trick in one brief session. Remember what I said about persistence being an important factor in the process. You need daily practice, day after day.

That question of practice has another benefit, incidentally. A lot of people find clear visualization difficult. If you're one of them, don't get disheartened. It's exactly like weight-lifting. Until your muscles develop, you can only manage little weights. But that doesn't mean you'll never be able to lift the heavy weights. It just means you need regular practice. Regular practice will develop your visualization muscles. Given time and practice, you'll find your visualizations become clearer and clearer.

Which is lucky for you. Because, as you'll see in the next chapter, visualization has a vital part to play in creating the circumstances for your personal success.

7

Defining Your Goals

There's a wise old saying that you should be careful what you pray for . . . in case your prayers are answered.

This is deeper than it sounds. Very often we have half-baked ideas of what we want. Even more often, when we think we know what we want, we don't take into consideration the consequences of getting it.

Shirley MacLaine, the film actress, wanted to be famous. Eventually she became famous. But then she resented the fact that she no longer had any privacy. People used to stop her in the street, insist on talking to her. She was, in a sense, no longer her own woman. It had not occurred to her that one consequence of fame had to be a loss of privacy. Maybe if it had, she wouldn't have wanted to be famous.

I had a client who wanted to run a particular kind of business. It wasn't an easy business, but it was the one he wanted. He worked hard and eventually made it. He was running the sort of business he's always wanted. But his marriage broke apart. Because of the long hours and dedication involved, because of frequent international travel and several other factors, it was a consequence of running that sort of business that he spent very little time with his wife and children. So his marriage broke apart.

There are endless examples of this sort of thing. You probably see a few around you. The moral is simple: when you step onto the road to personal success, make sure you know *exactly* where it's leading. Make sure you've figured out the consequences of the route you propose to take. And make sure you're happy about those consequences.

All of which adds up to *defining your goals*.

Every time I talk to people about defining their goals, I have this funny feeling I shouldn't be talking at all. Even now, I have the feeling I shouldn't be writing this chapter. It seems such a waste of time. Surely everybody knows what they want? They might not know how to get it, but at least they surely know what they want? Funny feelings aside, long experience has convinced me most people don't. Try asking your friends. Ask them to name the one thing they most want in the whole world, no holds barred. Then see how long it takes for them to give you an answer—especially a serious answer.

The fact of the matter is, most people don't take time to consider what they want out of life. They drift. They live one day, then another. Things happen to them, but they very seldom actually make things happen. There was an East European philosopher called Gurdjieff who came to the conclusion that most people went through life asleep. It may sound hard to believe, put like that, but when you look around you, most people live at a level where they might as well be sleepwalkers. Certainly their control over their destiny is very limited indeed.

Goal defining takes you out of this situation. Because, before you can start to make things happen, you need to know what it is you want to make happen.

Write Down Your List of Goals
What do you want to make happen? Where do you want to go? What do you want to become? There's only one way to tackle this. Get yourself a paper and pencil. Sit down right now and write out a list of your goals. Don't try to put them in any order of preference: just write them as they come into your head. At this stage you needn't go into detail. If you want a big house, just write down:

1. Big house.

Or maybe:

1. Big house in country.

Nothing more than that at this stage. All we're doing is getting you accustomed to a new way of thinking.

There is one rule I want to mention before you make your list. When you're making it, *you must not limit yourself in any way whatsoever*. If one of your goals is to make £500 billion, put it down, no matter how crazy it sounds. If one of your goals is to be on the next rocket to the moon, put it down. No limitations whatsoever. Look on it as a fun exercise.

But don't fool yourself that because it's a fun exercise it's an unimportant exercise. Nothing's further from the truth. This exercise is so important to your future that I'm going to make it easy for you. I'm going to make sure you don't have any excuse for passing over it. Instead of hunting round for a piece of paper to write on—which you're probably going to lose tomorrow anyway—I'm going to leave room for you to write your goals down right here in this book. That way you can refer back to them in the days ahead.

COMPREHENSIVE GOAL LIST

1	16 ....
2	17 ....
3	18 ....
4	19 ....
5	20 ....
6	21 ....
7	22 ....
8	23 ....
9	24 ....
10	25 ....
11	26 ....
12	27 ....
13	28 ....
14	29 ....
15	30 ....

I've left you thirty spaces. If you don't have thirty goals, don't start worrying about it. Just write down as many as you do have and leave the rest blank. But remember, don't limit yourself in any way. If it turns out you have more than thirty goals, that's all right too. Just list the rest on a separate sheet of paper and keep it inside this book.

Write those goals down *now* before you read any further. When you've finished, come back to this point and I'll tell you want to do next.

*   *   *

Okay, so now you've written down your goals. Some of them may be pretty simple and straightforward, like wanting a better job. Some of them may be a little silly, like wanting to be an engine driver, as you did when you were a kid. Some of them may seem pretty wild, like discovering an oil-well, or shooting Niagara Falls in a plastic dustbin. But no matter how silly they seem at this point in time, believe me they're okay. They're *your* goals and you're not answerable to anybody else for them. If you feel a bit coy, a bit embarrassed about any of them, ask yourself the question I used to ask my patients. Ask yourself, *Who's making my rules?*

Your next step in goal defining is a bit more difficult. I want you to go through that whole list carefully and think about the consequences of achieving each of those goals. This is going to take more time than it took to write the goals down, because I want you to do it very carefully indeed. I want you to imagine your situation as if you had already achieved that particular goal. I want you to figure out what the consequences would be. You don't have to write anything down this time. Do the work in your head, but be sure you do it thoroughly. If any of the goals presents a set of consequences you don't like, see if there's any way of achieving the goal while avoiding those consequences. If there's no way of avoiding the consequences, decide whether you're prepared to live with them for the sake of the goal.

When you've finished doing this, you'll find most of your goals will stand. But some won't. Some of them will have consequences you simply aren't prepared to face. When you find a goal like that, strike it out and forget about it. Once you've struck out the goals you no longer want, list the remainder down in the spaces below. But this time list them in order of preference.

AMENDED GOAL LIST

1	11 ....
2	12 ....
3	13 ....
4	14 ....
5	15 ....
6	16 ....
7	17 ....
8	18 ....
9	19 ....
10	20 ....

So now you know the goals you really want to achieve. And you know the first goal is the *most important goal of your life.* That's the one you're going to work hardest to achieve. And when you've achieved it, you know the second most important goal, and so on.

Don't worry if your goals aren't all about material things. In fact, those could easily be your most important goals. If they're not, that's fine too. Your goals are your own, your priorities are your own and you don't have to answer to anybody else for them.

Now the real work starts. Although you may not believe it for some time yet, you're about to take the first step towards achieving your goals. We're going to start with your first five, one at a time.

Go back to your amended goal list and look at what you've written for the first goal. I don't know what it is, of course, but let's suppose you've written something like:

1. Making a lot of money.

You've already figured out the consequences of making a lot of money and you're happy enough about facing them. So, making a lot of money is your first goal, the most important goal in your life at the moment. And it's an okay goal because you don't have to answer to anybody else for it.

But as it stands, it's too vague to take action on. You have to take that first goal and spell it out in detail. You have to work out, in detail, what your first goal really means. You have to figure out how long you're going to give yourself to achieve it.

1. Making a lot of money.

How much money is 'a lot?' £100? £1,000? £10,000? A million? Two million? You're the one to decide. Do you want the money in a lump sum, or spread out? Do you want to make a million? Or do you really want to make £20,000 a year for life? Don't limit yourself, but do get reality into that goal. Be literal. Imagine you were talking to your bank manager about a loan. He wouldn't be very impressed if you asked him vaguely for a 'lot of money'. He'd want to know how much, to the penny. And how you wanted it. And whether you wanted it in sterling, dollars or Swiss francs.

And while you're at it, decide how you want to make it. As an executive? As an entrepreneur? As a film producer? As an author? Or what? Finally, decide how long you're going to give yourself to achieve that goal. Six months? A year? Five years? Ten years? Try to be reasonable with this one. I've told you your limitations are imaginary, and I'll stick by that. But I've also told you some things are just plain impossible. Getting hold of £100 billion in crisp new one pound notes within five minutes from now is just plain impossible. It would take them longer than that just to count it out for you. So be reasonable about the time factor. When you've finished working out the detail, write down your first goal as fully as possible. It might go something like this:

1. Within three years, I want to be making £100,000 a year, after taxes, as general manager of an electrical goods manufacturing chain in Germany.

That's tying it down. Now tie down your own first goal, in as much detail as it needs, using the space below.

GOAL ONE   Date . . . .

. . . .
. . . .
. . . .
. . . .
. . . .
. . . .
. . . .

You'll notice I've left space for a date. Put today's date in there, the date you first accurately specified your first goal.

Your second goal might be simpler. You might, for example, have written:

2. A big car.

Once again, work out what that means in detail. How big is 'big'? What make of car do you want? What colour? Any optional extras? New or second hand? When you've figured out the details, you might put them down something like this:

2. Within eighteen months, I want to own a white Jaguar automatic, with air conditioning, electric windows and quadrophonic cassette player.

Now write down your own second goal, using the space below:

GOAL TWO   Date . . . .

. . . .
. . . .
. . . .
. . . .
. . . .
. . . .
. . . .

Maybe your third goal is the sort that's difficult to spell out clearly. But this just means a little extra work. You might, for example, have written:

3. Promotion.

Now promotion isn't a thing. It's not like money, which you can visualize in any shape from gold bricks to banknotes. It's not like a new car, which you can visualize from the alloy wheels to the tuck-away headlamps. Promotion isn't solid, so you need to know exactly what you mean by it. How far do you want to go? Where do you want to end up? Think about it carefully. Maybe you'd end up spelling it out something like this:

3. Inside a year, I want to be general manager of the company which employs me now. Within three years, I'd like to be a director of our main competitors, which is a bigger, more progressive firm.

See what I mean? Now fill in your own third, fourth and fifth goals in the spaces provided.

GOAL THREE   Date . . . .

. . . .
. . . .
. . . .
. . . .
. . . .
. . . .
. . . .

GOAL FOUR   Date . . . .

. . . .
. . . .
. . . .
. . . .
. . . .
. . . .
. . . .

GOAL FIVE   Date . . . .

. . . .
. . . .
. . . .
. . . .
. . . .
. . . .
. . . .

So much for your first five goals (I haven't forgotten the rest—we'll come to them in a minute. Right now, I'm taking things a step at a time for the sake of clarity). Now let's make a start on achieving them.

Achieving Your Goals
Tonight when you're visualizing during the hypnogogic period, throw in a quick visualization of your first goal. Later, when you've mastered the trick of total relaxation at will, I want you to devote a special time each day to goal

visualization. Pick five minutes when you know you won't be interrupted—morning's best—and visualize your goal in detail. This won't be so hard to do now, since you've already broken down your first five goals into detail. If you're visualizing Goal 2, for instance, you know you're to visualize a white Jag and you know how it looks inside.

And here's the trick. Visualize the situation *as if you had already achieved the goal in question*. See yourself driving that lovely white Jag. Imagine your hands on the wheel. Visualize yourself playing a cassette. Listen mentally to the quality of sound coming from those four speakers. See the road ahead of you, the scenery each side of you. Get the feel of the car. Visualize clearly and carefully so you end up knowing every last inch of that car, every peculiarity of the way it handles. See the places you'll go to in it. See yourself enjoying it.

If it's promotion you're after, see yourself enjoying the results of promotion. See yourself at your new desk in your new office, doing your new work.

In other words, show your unconscious mind clearly what it is you want. Get your unconscious on your side, so it works for you instead of against you. Take one visualization and work on it each and every day. You don't have to spend very long, especially after you've mastered the trick of visualizing clearly and in detail. Keep working on the visualization until things begin to happen. I can't tell you how long that will take, because it depends on what it is you want to achieve and how long you've set yourself to achieve it. But I can tell you that, given time, total relaxation, and constant daily visualization, things *will* begin to happen. I know this from personal experience and from the experience of others who have tried the method. I don't know why it works, only that it does. But I have some speculations.

It seems to me that most of us, psychologists included, greatly undervalue the abilities of the unconscious mind. It seems to me your unconscious mind is a giant, with hidden abilities we're only just beginning to guess at. It's like having Superman as a partner, except that most of the time you don't bother to talk to him, so that most of the time he lets you go your own way. But once you start to talk to him consistently, once you convince him about the things you want, all of a sudden he puts his super-powers to work and starts arranging things to fit in with your plans.

This is a very simple, almost naive model, but it's useful. Because you're going to find the breaks really do start coming in your direction once you're visualizing properly and consistently. And that can be a little scary if you don't know what's going on. So when things start to happen, don't get uptight and panic. Remind yourself of what you've been doing. You've been hoisting signals to your unconscious mind, and now that sleeping giant has woken up and started to help you do the things you want to do.

Work through your visualizations in sequence, writing them down in detail as you did for the first five, visualizing them in detail, day after day. You can run through three or

GOAL CHECK LIST

Goal Number	Date set	Date achieved
1		
2		
3		
4		
5		
6		
7		
8		
9		
10		
11		
12		
13		
14		
14		
15		
16		
17		
18		
19		
20		

four in a single visualization session. Or you can work away doggedly at one until that one cracks, then go on to the next. But keep at it. And report the results in the space opposite.

Just to give you a little extra confidence in this technique, I'm going to show you a little of the power of your unconscious mind. I'm going to show you a technique which will prove the power of your unconscious mind inside two weeks at the very most. It's a technique you can start using right away. It's a technique which you will keep using for the rest of your life, because the results are so worthwhile and fantastic. It's a technique which you can learn as quickly as it takes you to read the next chapter.

8

Your Mental Computer

Amazing what computers can do nowadays. They've been programmed to play bridge and chess. There was even a chess match between a Russian and an American computer. (The Russian computer won.) They can handle complex calculations in a fraction of a second. They can direct traffic. They can talk to you. They can store an amount of information you wouldn't believe possible. But even the best of them hasn't the capacity of the biological computer inside your skull. Whatever may happen in the future, at this moment in time, brains are still best—provided you know how to use them.

If your brain was a mechanical computer and you were a computer technician, you'd be appalled at how inefficiently it was used. You'd know the amazing potential of this computer, and you'd know only a fraction of that potential ever gets to do anybody any good. The trouble is, learning to use the biological computer takes a bit of time and a bit of effort. Most people never bother. Which, as I remarked earlier, is why most people never achieve personal success.

In this chapter, you're going to learn how to use your biological computer more efficiently. It will take time and effort (although less of both than you probably imagine), but I think you'll agree the results are going to be well worthwhile. Especially since I can demonstrate some of those results very quickly. When you've learned the techniques in this chapter, you won't have learned everything there is to know about using your brain. Not by a long chalk. But you will have learned something very useful indeed on your road to personal success. Because using your brain even a little more efficiently than the next man will mark you out of the herd. Believe me, the man who uses his brain efficiently stands out like a beacon in a competitive situation.

I'm going to begin by teaching you how to use your storage retrieval process. Which is computer jargon for learning how to improve your memory.

How's your memory at the moment? Chances are you think it's pretty poor. But let me assure you of something that will surprise you. Your memory is brilliant. Almost miraculous, in fact. Your only problem is, you don't know how to use it.

One of the world's greatest living experts on the art of memory is America's Harry Lorrayne. He's on record as saying very few people actively forget anything. It's just that they don't take the trouble to remember in the first place. That sounds contradictory, but it isn't. When you're introduced to someone at a party, do you really make an effort to remember the name? If you're like most people, you probably don't even hear the name properly; and you're too shy to ask to have it repeated. Too shy . . . or too lazy. As Harry Lorrayne says, you don't make any effort to remember in the first place.

But even when you do make an effort, memory probably doesn't come all that easily to you. Remember when you were learning poetry and formulae and history dates at school? You really had to strain to get anything to stick in your head. You had to go over the thing again and again.

I have good news for you. That was the hard way to remember. It was also the worst way.

The secret of each memory is very, very old. So old that the ancient Greeks knew it. But for some reason it fell into disuse. The art of memory was one of the occult arts around the time of the Renaissance, which means that only a few people ever knew about it. As time went on, it ceased to be taught even to occultists. As a result, we now live in an age when poor memory is normal. We accept it as a fact of life.

Businessmen make notes of their appointments in diaries. Filing cabinets bulge to capacity. Executives dictate memos to themselves on miniature tape recorders. A whole technology has come into being to prop up human memory. But poor memory is not a fact of life. Because the memory secret was never actually lost. It fell into disuse, but it never actually vanished altogether.

The memory secret, like so much else of value in this book, depends on your use of visual imagination. There's no way I can teach you the full art of memory in a single chapter. That would take a book all on its own. But I can teach you the basic principles. Enough to show you the marvellous memory feats that are within your grasp. Enough to set you apart from your fellow businessmen. Enough to let you throw away some of the memory props most people have to use. And if you want to go further, there are other books on the market, easily obtainable, which will give you the full story.

The Secret of the Memory Locus
So, let's spell out one of the basic principles. I'll start with a principle which was known and used by Renaissance occultists and by the ancient Greeks before them.

This is the principle of the *locus*.

Locus means place. And in the art of memory, a locus is the place you put things you want to remember. It's a place that exists inside your skull, in the realms of visual imagination. To start building up a trained memory, you must first build up your locus. In Renaissance times, the most popular loci were buildings, the bigger the better. Had you lived then, you might have spotted an occultist muttering his way through some public building as he worked to establish its corridors and colonnades as his personal memory locus.

For the Renaissance occultist, this was often a difficult job, because he aimed at achieving a truly miraculous memory— one that could help him recite whole books verbatim and memorize long-winded rituals full of barbaric names and foreign phrases. That required a very extensive locus indeed. In your own case, it's unlikely that you'll be quite so ambitious— or that you'll ever need to be quite so ambitious. So your locus can be a lot smaller. Which is going to save you a lot of effort at the beginning. In fact, your locus almost certainly exists already. It's just that you've never thought of using it as a memory aid.

Let's see if we can find a good locus for you. The Renaissance idea of a building is first class, so we'll stick to it. Sit back for a moment and decide on a building you already know well. Your home, maybe, or your office, or a friend's home, or perhaps even a public building you've visited so often, so extensively, that you know every nook and cranny of it. Now make a picture of that building in your mind. Imagine yourself going in through the front door and visiting each of the rooms in turn. Try to see this as clearly as possible. Make the visualization as detailed as possible.

Practice doing this a few times. But make sure you always visit the imaginary rooms in the same sequence each time. This is very important, so don't neglect it. Establish a route through the house and *always* stick to the same order in the rooms you visit. When you can undertake this visualization with ease, when the route you take through the house is second nature to you, your locus is ready for use.

Here's how to use it:

Let's assume that, for some reason or other, you want to remember the following list:

1. Door key
2. Typewriter
3. Motor car
4. Box of cigars
5. Filing cabinet
6. The Dictionary
7. Electric cooker
8. Top hat
9. Stuffed badger
10. Willow tree
11. Egyptian mummy
12. Model aeroplane
13. Pipe rack
14. Vacuum cleaner
15. Space ship
16. String of sausages
17. Lady's evening dress

18. Sea-shell
19. The Mona Lisa
20. A shrunken head.

I've deliberately made up the list of items which have absolutely no logical connection with each other. In other words, I've made the list as difficult as possible to remember. If you were to shut your eyes right now and try to remember that list, you might get a few items, but I doubt if you'd manage to remember the whole twenty. If you had to recite the list in the order given, you'd probably do even less well. Yet by using your locus, you can remember the entire list with very little effort. And you can remember it in order. Or reverse order, if you really want to impress your friends.

This is how it works:

Visualize your building locus. Go up to the front door and imagine a big key sticking in the lock. See this clearly in your mind's eye.

Go through the door and imagine a big typewriter in the front hall. Maybe on the floor, so you almost trip over it.

Following your familiar route, go into the first room and visualize your astonishment when you find a full-sized motor car in there, parked up by the fireplace. How on Earth did they get it in?

On to the next place on your route, and there visualize a box of cigars. When you're dealing with smallish objects like this, it's as well to exaggerate them. So make the box big. See yourself taking out a fat cigar and light it (if you don't smoke, visualize it making you cough).

Then on to the next room, where you find a filing cabinet propped up against an armchair.

Getting the hang of it? It's a very simple system. Simply keep moving through your locus, visualizing the various objects on the list in the various places you visit. If the objects themselves are small, exaggerate them in size. Do this until you've placed every object on the list.

But suppose your locus doesn't have twenty rooms — what then? There's actually no need to use up a whole room for a single item. You can place two or more items in different places in a room. But make sure you place the items in order along the route you habitually take through that room.

For example, your first object (say the top hat) would be placed just inside the door of the room. If your habitual route through the room takes you to a table in the centre, then over to the window, then across to the fireplace, then over the hearth rug, then out through a second door, you can use each of these sub-divisions as a resting place for the objects on your list. The stuffed badger goes on the table, the willow tree has fallen through the window, the mummy is propped up against the fireplace, the model aeroplane has crashed on the hearth rug and so on.

Once you've placed every object on your list along the route you take through your locus, you've done the job you set out to do. You've memorized that difficult, illogical, complicated list in its entirety. When you want to recall the list in order, you simply walk through your imaginary locus again calling out what you see there. If you want the list in reverse order, you simply reverse your route.

The odd thing about this system is that once you place an object in a locus room, it stays there without any effort until you consciously make the effort to throw it out (thus making room for new objects from another list). And it will stay there as long as you need it. With a little practice, you can place the objects in your locus in no more time than it takes someone to read the list through once, aloud. The result is an impressive memory feat when you reel the list right back afterwards.

As you become accustomed to using your locus, you can dream up all sorts of useful modifications. You might, for instance, build on a reminder room. In this room, under a flashing warning light, you can place the one thing you must not forget to do that day. Then, when you're wondering what on earth it was your wife (or your boss, if the two happen to be different) asked you to do, you can slip briefly into your reminder room and there will be the information you want.

The Link Technique

There's another method of remembering that list, without the use of a locus. This technique too uses visual imagination and is the one more often taught in modern memory training. It's called the *link* technique, and this is how it works:

Take the first item on your list (the door key) and make a ridiculous association between it and the second item (the typewriter). Visualize the result. Now make a ridiculous association between typewriter and motor car. Visualize the result. Now between motor car and cigar box. Once again, visualize the result. And so on, to the end of your list.

Let me give you an example of what I mean. You've started with door key and you want to associate it in a ridiculous manner with typewriter. You might visualize yourself trying to type a letter on a door key. Or trying desperately to open your front door with a typewriter. The more ludicrous the association the better. Once you've made the picture in your mind, forget it and move on to the next. But do make sure you see that picture clearly in your mind's eye. Having associated door key with typewriter, you now have to associate typewriter with motor car. You might picture yourself driving down an open highway in a typewriter. Imagine the odd looks you're getting from passing motorists.

Car to cigar box is easy. You can see your car stuffed full of cigars. See yourself painfully opening the top up to get one. And so it goes on, until you've associated your way through the entire list. Oddly enough, once you've done that (remembering to visualize clearly and make the associations really ludicrous), the rest is automatic. As you start to repeat the list, you'll find the minute door key comes into your head, it drags typewriter behind it. And that drags up the motor car. And that pulls along the cigar box. Everything comes up in the right order, like links of a chain—hence the name of the method.

You'll find with this method, too, running the list backwards is no more difficult than running it forwards. Again the process is totally automatic, once you've done the work of making the visualized associations.

Take time out to test the method now. Use either or both techniques and see how easily memorizing that 'difficult' list has become now. From being able to recall one or two items, you'll now be able to reel off the entire list of twenty without a single mistake. And it would make no difference if you doubled, or even trebled the number of items. So long as you visualize clearly and make really ludicrous associations, so long as your locus is big enough, there doesn't seem to be any real limit to the number of things you can remember.

When you've tried out this new use of your storage retrieval system, come back to me and I'll let you in on another secret use of your biological computer. One that's going to let you solve the most difficult problems without an ounce of conscious effort.

*   *   *

What you're going to learn now is a problem-solving technique so simple, so easy, that you're not going to believe it will really work until you try it.

It's the technique of solving problems in your sleep. That's right, in your sleep. Furthermore, the solutions you're going to get will amost invariably be better than the ones you'd come up with by worrying round the problem while awake. There's a reason for this. The problems aren't solved by magic. They're solved by your own unconscious mind. Remember what I said about the unconscious mind being a giant? It's also a bit of a genius. It has a vast wealth of experience to draw on, and it thinks differently from the way you do (consciously). As a result, you get a fresh slant on your problems—and some unexpected types of solution.

You'd imagine with a simple, easy technique like this, everybody would be using it. I can't help feeling that at one time nearly everybody did. You still frequently hear people talking about 'sleeping on' a difficult decision. Somehow they feel things will be clearer in the morning. But if you ask them why, they'll say it's because they're fresher in the morning, or some similar excuse. In fact, just 'sleeping on' a problem sometimes works quite well, but sometimes doesn't shed any light on the matter at all. This is pretty useless to the man in search of personal success. He wants a problem-solving mechanism he can rely on, time after time. And that's just the mechanism I'm going to give you now. Maybe, as I said, everybody used it at one time, but like the memory secret it gradually fell out of favour. But, again like the memory secret, it wasn't lost completely. You can start using it tonight. You can keep using it every night of your life.

The way it works is this:

Let's assume you're faced with a commonplace business problem. You have an important job out to tender and you've been landed with two identical quotes. Both quotes come from reputable firms. You've never had work done by either, but you've checked into the background of each and found they tended to take slightly different approaches to your type of job. One works slowly, but very carefully. The other works faster, but with slightly less attention to detail. And that's your problem. A fast job is going to save you money on the contract, which makes you favour firm B. But you can't afford to have even the slightest mistake made on the job, which makes you favour firm A. There's no difference in the costings, so you can't use that as a guide. You're stuck with the problem and you simply can't make up your mind.

From now on, in these circumstances, you turn the problem over to your biological computer. You do so in the following sequence:

First, gather up all the information you can about the problem. Doesn't matter whether it seems particularly relevant to the solution or not, just find out as much as possible about each of those two firms.

Next, make one last conscious attempt to solve your problem without calling in the biological computer. If you succeed, great. If not, proceed to the next step.

Next, just before you fall asleep, go over the problem in your mind, trying to visualize the situation. This may not be all that easy, for some problems are quite abstract. Don't get hung up about the difficulty. Just visualize those parts of the problem which lend themselves to visualization.

Finally, visualize yourself waking up in the morning with the solution to your problem.

And that's it! That's the whole process from beginning to end! So simple, you can hardly believe it, can you? But don't knock it till you try it. The notebook and pencil by your bedside is for you to write down the solution as early as possible after you wake up. Sometimes a sleepy, early morning mind has a way of forgetting the solutions by the time you're up and ready for the morning toast. So write down the solution immediately.

And suppose no solution has presented itself? I have to admit that sometimes happens—especially in the early days, before you have the technique off pat. The answer is, go through the same process the following night. And, if necessary, the night after that. I've used the biological computer in this way for years, and I can't remember a single problem that couldn't be cracked within a week this way. Most of them only take a night or two; and an appreciable percentage can be worked out in a single session.

I want you to use your biological computer. I want you to get accumstomed to using it. Once you've got the hang of it, you've finished your preparations for success.

In the next section of this book, you'll learn a few tips you can use on the road to success itself.

PART TWO

The Principles of Power Play

The techniques in this section are directly related to business success. Learn them, enjoy them, but, above all, *use* them.

They're the techniques which will turn all the hard work you've put into the first section of this book into a dynamic power-packed programme for personal success in the world of business.

9

Getting An Interview

For over a year in the 1960s, a friend of mine, with less scruples than most, managed to make a living as a professional interviewee.

Each day, and each weekend, he'd buy up all the best papers and carefully go through the Situations Vacant columns. He wasn't looking for a job (in a sense, he'd got one already and was at that moment working at it). He was looking for situations which promised to pay an applicant's expenses if he was called for an interview. When he found one, he'd carefully cut it out and put it in a file. Each night, he'd take out the file and write a letter of application for every post in the advertisements he'd collected that day. It didn't matter to him whether the job was general manager of a laundry, or assistant director of a chemical research institute. It didn't matter to him whether the post called for knowledge of a dozen different languages, including Urdu and Swahili, or the qualifications of a nuclear physicist. He applied for them all.

In a week or two, back would come the replies. Could he please present himself for an interview? He could—and did. After his early morning session with the Situations Vacant columns, his day was spent attending interviews. At the end of each, he'd present his bill for expenses. Travel, meals and other incidentals. When he left, he'd enough cash to live on for another day.

It was a precarious existence, and one I wouldn't, frankly, recommend. But the interesting thing about it was that my friend, who did not speak Urdu and wouldn't know one end of an atom from the other, was able consistently to land interviews for the best jobs in the country. He was able to land interviews day after day. His livelihood actually depended on this one talent. I know a lot of very well-qualified business executives and professional men who would give their right arms for that talent. Despite their education, background and experience, they're stuck in dead-end jobs. And while they're anxious to get out and net themselves something better, they somehow never manage it. As often as not, they don't even get to first base. As often as not, they receive a negative reply to their requests for an interview.

Where are they going wrong? Where are they missing out? Why do highly suitable applicants fail to get an interview, while a man with no qualifications at all can produce a positive response time after time? Are we to blame the companies which run the ads? Can we conclude that their personnel managers are fools? It's hardly likely. But even if it were true, that's little consolation to the man applying for the job. If he doesn't get an interview — for whatever reason — he doesn't get the job. And that's the end of that.

When a man is turned down for interview after interview, a sense of desperation creeps in. He begins to take more time over his letters of application. He makes them more detailed, more comprehensive. He polishes the style to make it more impressive. But still he doesn't get the interviews.

If you're in that situation, I've good news for you. It's *easy* to get an interview when you know how. Without long letters. Without polished style. Without taking a great deal of time and trouble. What's even better news is that your initial application can be so powerful that it virtually ensures you have the job before they even see you. That may sound exaggerated, but it's not. The man who taught me how to write letters of application successfully netted his first interview — and his first job — on the basis of a letter which ran to four words. That's right, *four words*. What's more, they weren't even neatly typed. They were scrawled, in ink, across a piece of paper torn out of a newspaper.

Let me give you the full history of that remarkable letter. Because it illustrates the technique of landing an interview. Or at least illustrates one of the techniques.

At the time, the man in question had set his sights on a job as an advertising copywriter with one of the larger agencies. He was young, and he had no previous experience. Copywriting is a very specialist skill (I know, because I've done it) and agencies are very hesitant to take on anybody who hasn't proved himself. There's a lot of money involved, even in the smallest account, and a poor piece of copy, a wrong creative idea, can lose an account faster than a ferret disappearing down a rabbit hole. So you can see the situation for my friend wasn't exactly hopeful. If he'd sat down and written a formal letter of application, nicely laid out and carefully typed, I'd be prepared to bet my numbered Swiss account he'd have got exactly the same thing back — a nicely laid out, carefully typed, formal letter of rejection.

But he didn't write a formal letter of application. Instead, he bided his time. And while he was waiting, he took a course in copywriting. Now, education's a grand thing and academic qualifications are often essential, for certain jobs. But the particular copywriting course my friend took wasn't a particularly good one (although it was the only one available). Inside the agencies, nobody was very impressed by that particular course. If you took it, that showed you were enthusiastic, but nobody thought it actually did very much for you in the way of training.

At the same time, the course ended with a copywriting competition. My friend entered and came first. The fact was picked up by the local paper, which ran a short item giving his name and address and the fact that he'd come first in the copywriting competition. And when that happened, my friend made his move. He tore the report out of the paper and scrawled four words across it:

'This gun for hire.'

Then he posted it off to the agency. By the end of the week, he had a job.

Why was the agency so impressed by this crazy 'letter' of application? Because it showed imagination? Well . . . yes.

Because it showed originality? Well . . . that too. But the main reason why they were impressed was that my friend took the trouble of actually *showing* them what he could do instead of just *telling* them what he could do.

What's more, he didn't waste their time in the process (how long does it take to read four words?). He was direct, to the point. And, most important of all, he was thinking in terms of the company, not in terms of himself. The letter was written in a way an advertising agency would appreciate.

When you can do that, you're a long way towards netting an interview—not just with an advertising agency, but with any company at all.

The Method

Let's get down to business right now and analyse in detail how you should go about getting a job interview. Obviously, the exact approach will vary slightly, depending on the type of job you're after. But the principles won't. In fact, the method I'm about to spell out can be used to net you an interview for any job whatsoever. I have used it personally. I've taught it to clients and friends. It very seldom fails, because getting an interview is one of the easiest parts of getting a job.

First of all, how do you know a job is open? There are three possibilities. 1) The grapevine. 2) An employment agency. 3) The Press. In certain specialist fields, the grapevine is the best (and often the only) means of obtaining information about job opportunities. If you're plugged in, fine. If you're not, get plugged in. You can do this by talking to people in the business. But talk to them regularly, and don't hesitate to mention you're in search of employment. There's no need to be coy. If people don't know what you're after, they're unlikely to give you the information you need, even with the best will in the world. Employment agencies may do a fine job, but if I were hunting for employment, I'd only use them in the direst emergency. If an agency is involved in vetting applications for an advertised job, I tend to shy away—or at least approach the whole thing with an air of despondency and gloom. You'll see why in a moment. The richest harvest of job opportunities, as my friend the professional employee discovered, is in the Situations Vacant columns of a newspaper. Go through them carefully, looking for a job that suits you. And while you're going through, remember that your limitations are imaginary. Don't pass up a good job that suits your talents just because you think you mightn't be able to handle it. Get your application in and let the company worry about your abilities.

Let's assume for a while you've seen a job you fancy advertised in the paper. Let's also assume no employment agency is involved. How do you go about getting an interview?

Somewhere in the ad—usually towards the end—you'll find instructions on how you should apply. Most companies ask for written applications. A few may require you to 'phone in. We can safely ignore those which request you call personally. This sort of approach almost always means you're being offered a low-paid, insecure type of job— piecework in a factory or on a building site, for instance. Alternatively, the company behind the ad might be involved in some of the more shady forms of direct selling. Neither should have much appeal for a man on the road to personal success. And besides, when personal calling is advocated, the mechanics of getting an interview obviously become irrelevant.

The first mistake most people make is assuming the instructions in the ad have the same weight as Holy Writ. They haven't. The receptionist in a firm managed by a colleague of mine landed her job precisely because she ignored the instructions in the application ad. My colleague had asked applicants to write first, giving details of age, education and experience. The girl 'phoned him directly, told him that since the job obviously involved dealing with 'phone callers she was giving him an opportunity to hear her 'phone voice and experience her 'phone manner. He was so impressed, he offered her the post on the spot—without even seeing her! He tells me he's never regretted the decision either.

A request for written details of 'age, education and experience' is a formula frequently used in advertising, because the advertiser can't think of anything better to say.

In certain circumstances, it may be usefully ignored. But only in certain circumstances. Many companies insist on a written application because their personnel officers are just too busy to deal with a flood of 'phone calls from prospects who may be useless for the post advertised. If you ignore the instruction in these circumstances, you may not even get through to the man you want. And if you do, you will have to face a certain amount of irritation that you've broken the rules.

So what are the circumstances in which you may actually give yourself an edge by breaking the rules?

First, and obviously, where the job involves a great deal of 'phone work, like the case of my colleague's receptionist, or a company which specializes in selling its wares by 'phone. You can do exactly what the girl did in my example. Ring through and explain *why* you're ringing instead of writing.

Second, where you have outstanding qualifications for the job. A 'phone call can short-circuit a lot of waiting around and marks you out as somebody different (all the other applicants will be busy following the rules). Your qualifications will usually outweigh any irritation your direct approach may cause.

Third, where you have supreme confidence in your ability to sell yourself over the 'phone (usually coupled with doubts about selling yourself through a letter).

Fourth, where the time element has made a letter impracticable. In this case, you should apologize for the direct approach and explain the reasons. Most companies will accept them without a second thought.

The edge you give yourself by direct action in these circumstances is twofold. First, you isolate yourself from the herd. You make yourself remembered. When an ad requires written application, the herd writes. But it may be the maverick who lands himself the job. Your second edge is psychological. It is always more difficult for someone to say 'no' to you directly than it is to turn you down via a letter. And bear in mind that you aren't 'phoning to ask for a job, you're only 'phoning to ask for an interview. Nine times out of ten you'll get it. The tenth time you'll probably be redirected to the writing route. *It very seldom happens that a*

direct approach will actually ruin your chances of the post.
This is worth bearing in mind.

But maybe your 'phone's broken down, or you've got laryngitis, or the circumstances aren't appropriate. How do you land an interview then? You write, that's how. And this is the way you write:

First off, read through the advertisement carefully and find out what your prospective employer says he wants. Most times he says he wants experience, education, a particular talent. Occasionally he says he wants enthusiasm.

Now think for a moment about what he *really* wants.

He wants somebody who can do the job. That's what he really wants. That's all he really wants. Everything he *says* he wants is just proof, or what he takes to be proof, that the applicant can do the job.

Ask yourself if you can do the job. Forget about education, experience and everything else the ad has stressed. Just ask yourself if you can do the job. If the answer's yes, ask yourself *why* the answer's yes. It may be that education, experience and the rest have all got something to do with your reasons why you can do the job. That's all to the good. But if these factors don't come into it, forget them. You're still qualified for the job, no matter what your prospective employer thinks. All you have to do is convince him. Keep that in mind when you sit down to write your application letter. And keep in mind something even more important at this stage. You aren't writing to ask for a job (which is a very big thing for any employer to give you). You're writing to ask for an interview. Let me repeat that:

You're writing to ask for an interview.

Once that's firmly in your mind, your whole attitude towards the letter changes for the better. You're no longer asking that faceless man for a job, which is going to cost his company thousands to give you. You're only asking for an interview, which is going to cost him half an hour of his time. It's not such a big thing you're asking, not such a big thing at all. Besides which, he's already invited you to reply, via the ad. Since you've decided you can handle the job, you're automatically one of the men he's looking for when he decided to place the ad.

All this is more than a psychological comfort mechanism. It's a conscious gearing of your mind to approach the application letter in the right way. Because most applicants waste a lot of time trying to tell the man why they should be given the *job*. And it is a waste of time. There's no way he's going to hand out the job on the basis of a letter, no matter how detailed or well written. He's going to want to see you first, face to face across his desk. But once you have firmly in mind that you're only asking for an interview, you can concentrate on the real essentials. Persuading him to give you an interview. Not a job, just an interview. This exercise in persuasion isn't that difficult. The man has paid out good money to advertise a post. To justify that expenditure, he needs a response. To find the best man for the post, he can't afford to ignore even a half-interesting prospect.

The Application Letter
Here's an example of an application letter which will land you an interview for almost any type of job advertised.

> Dear ....,
>
> Your advertisement intrigued me, because I can't help feeling I'm exactly the sort of man you need.
>
> I'd like the opportunity of explaining why. May I ring your secretary on Wednesday to arrange a mutually suitable appointment?
>
> Yours sincerely,

Two short paragraphs. No details of age, education, background or experience. Are you shocked to hear that two short paragraphs can land interviews when long, carefully-polished letters fail? You shouldn't be. Because a little analysis will show you why that letter works. And why it has worked, time and again. It's short, so it doesn't take up too much of a busy reader's time. It's subtly flattering because it tells him right away that he produced an intriguing advertisement. It says directly that you're the man he needs, without giving him an opportunity to make up his mind one way or the other (this is where a detailed letter often fails. The reader can decide there and then whether he feels the applicant is suitable for the job. But remember, you're not asking for a job; you're asking for an interview).

In the second paragraph, the letter asks directly and simply for an interview. Experience teaches that when you ask people clearly and directly for something, they will often give it to you. The second sentence of the second paragraph is almost Machiavellian in its cunning. It forces him to take action if he wants to turn down your very reasonable request. He is forced to write back and tell you NOT to ring his secretary on Wednesday. At the very least, he is forced to instruct his secretary to ignore your call. Since it's more difficult to take action than to allow matters to take their course, the chances swing right over to your side. Besides, as we've already noted, he actively wants to see prospects for the post. There's no reason (because you haven't given him one) why he should avoid seeing you.

So, having sent that letter, all you have to do is ring the secretary on Wednesday. Tell her you've been in contact with her boss, which is true, and that you're now 'phoning to arrange an interview with him.

You'll get it.

When you're applying for an interview, you can use the letter exactly as I've outlined it. Or you can make your own modifications to suit the particular circumstances. But if you modify, keep in mind the basic rules.

1. Keep the letter short. There's no reason why it should run over one page.

2. Ask for an interview, not for the job.

3. Explain why you should have an interview, not why you should have the job.

4. Make it easy for him to agree, by forcing him to take action should he decide to refuse.

5. Type the letter out neatly and cleanly, or have it typed out for you. Presentation is always important.

6. Follow through. That's vital. 'Phone his secretary on Wednesday, or whatever day you've specified. If you've suddenly fallen ill or ended up in hospital with a broken leg, make sure somebody else 'phones on your behalf. Not just to apologize, but to arrange the interview for when you get well.

By following these simple rules (or just by sending out my

sample letter) I can absolutely guarantee you will be granted far more interviews than you can handle.

Provided, that is, an employment agency is not involved. I have to come right out in the open and admit that this sort of approach is a waste of time where an agency is involved, because agencies have a standard form they require you to fill out, packed with standard questions about age, education and previous experience. When an agency's involved, you're forced to apply for the job and not for the interview. There are, frankly, only two ways round this. If you can find out the name of the principal company, write to them direct and short-circuit the agency. Be brash (and flattering)—explain that you prefer to deal directly with top men. Then ask for an *interview* as before. The second way around is to write directly to the head of the agency. Ask for an interview with him. Explain you're the best man for the job, but *refuse* to fill out forms. You don't have to explain your refusal. An interview with an agency head is a thousand miles away from an interview with the company who hired the agency. But if you're really desperate, it's worth a try.

*   *   *

By now, you may have detected an odd flavour about the approach I'm advocating. You'll have noticed it doesn't depend on the conservative way of doing things. It doesn't depend on qualifications, or experience. It doesn't depend on what you are, or really what you have to offer. It depends on analysis of the other man. It depends on handling the other man. It depends, to use a word that's not all that respectable these days, on *manipulating* the other man, using his own psychology against him so that he reacts in ways favourable to you. So far that's just a flavour. But it's a flavour which will grow stronger in the following chapters. It's the flavour of *Power Play*. And you'll taste it often on your road to personal success.

10

Power Play At The Interview

So you've landed your interview. The big day's arrived. You're clean and polished and shaking with nerves. You're wondering what he's going to ask, and you're wondering what you're going to say.

His secretary shows you in. He comes round from behind his desk and shakes your hand. You exchange the usual formalities. He doesn't look like an ogre exactly, but you're still nervous. You feel clumsy. You stand around until he invites you to sit down, then you sit down. You wait.

'Well now, Mr . . . ah—' He checks a file and finds your name. He smiles at you. 'You're interested in joining us, I see.'

You nod. 'Yes.'

He nods. 'Well, perhaps you could tell me something about your background?'

So you tell him about your education and the jobs you've done and the posts you've held. Then you stop. He asks you about your outside interests. Do you play golf? Have you any hobbies? That sort of thing. You tell him yes or no, as appropriate. He asks you if you have anything else you particularly want to tell him. You think for a moment, then hesitantly admit that there's nothing. He tells you he has other applicants to see and promises to let you know the decision. He thanks you for coming. He shakes your hand again. He sees you out.

The whole thing's taken maybe fifteen minutes.

That's the typical interview scene. When you've been through it, you spend an hour or two analysing how you've done. You think maybe he was impressed by your background, but he seemed disappointed that you don't play golf. You don't know if you'll get the job, but you hope you will. It never occurs to you that you've missed a golden opportunity. It never occurs to you that you've handled it badly, that you've done just about everything wrong. It never occurs to you that the interview was an almost total waste of time. And the fact that most other applicants will have behaved exactly as you did, is precious little consolation.

You made your first mistake *before* you walked in through that office door. You made it in your head. You'd applied for a job as (say) manager of one of the company's chain of dry cleaning shops. So you thought the interview was about your experience of management, or about your experience of dry cleaning.

It wasn't. The interview was about *selling*. To be precise, the interview was about *selling yourself*.

That's the interview secret. The sole, central interview secret. It doesn't matter what sort of job you're after, from managing director to office boy, from dry cleaning shops to international oil companies. In every case, without exception, the interview is about selling yourself. Sell yourself successfully, and you've got the job. Fail to sell yourself, and you haven't. It's as simple as that.

The man who practices *Power Play* knows all about selling himself. In fact, he knows he had already started to sell himself even before he walked into the interview office. He wrote a short, confident letter of application, well-typed on good notepaper. It was an unusual letter of application, and because it was unusual it marked him out as an unusual applicant. The interviewer had to be intrigued about this applicant. The interviewer had to be wondering what sort of man would write such a short, confident letter. An interviewer who's intrigued is an interviewer who's already half sold.

How can *you* apply the principles of *Power Play* to the interview situation? Simply by following the instructions laid out, step by step, in the remainder of this chapter.

*   *   *

Power Play begins before you attend the interview. It begins the day you get word that your application for an interview has been granted. And it begins inside your head.

The successful job applicant is a confident applicant. Since you've already worked your way through Part One of this book, your confidence level is already pretty high. But it will do no harm to boost your confidence with relation to the particular situation you're facing. And that, once again, means visualization.

Each day, from the day you're notified about the interview to the day of the interview itself, put aside five minutes for a special confidence visualization. Get yourself totally relaxed (I'm assuming that by this time you've achieved the trick of total relaxation). Then visualize as follows:

See yourself walking confidently into the interview. See yourself charming and relaxed. See yourself subtly taking control of the interview. See yourself handling that interview flawlessly. And finally, see the interviewer offering you the job. You won't be able to make this visualization as accurately detailed as usual, of course. Almost certainly you won't know in advance what your interviewer looks like, or what his office looks like. But don't let this worry you. Make a guess at both and use your guess to build up the picture. In this case the really important focus of the visualization is *you*. So get detail into that aspect. Get detail into the mental picture of the way you look and the confident way you behave.

By the time your interview comes along, your unconscious mind will know how you want it handled. Given enough time, you can use this method to visualize yourself into a state of utter confidence, so that 'interview nerves' don't get a chance to spoil your chances.

But suppose you don't have time for this visualization programme? Suppose your notification is delayed and you've only a day or two, perhaps only a few hours, to prepare for your interview? There are still emergency methods you can use for stopping interview nerves dead in their tracks.

You might, for instance, use the breathing method. The great benefit of this technique is that it can be used anywhere, anytime. You don't need privacy, you don't need to lie down, you don't need to engage in any elaborate ritual. Use it when the butterflies start. And keep using it each time they come back. It's not a cure for nerves, simply a temporary panacea. This is what you do:

Empty your lungs completely. People very seldom do this, although most people imagine they do when they breathe out. To empty your lungs completely requires a drawing in of the stomach muscles. So press in with your stomach and get all the dead air out of your lungs. Now breathe in slowly and deeply. Take in as much fresh air as you can without straining.

Now hold your breath for a moment. And finally, breathe out fast. If you happen to be alone at the time, you can afford to breathe out explosively, which is the best way of all in this exercise. But breathing out explosively makes a noise, so if you're in company, you'll have to make do with breathing out fast.

If the butterflies don't go at the first attempt, repeat the exercise up to three times.

Another method you can use is the *exaggeration method*. This one is going to sound silly, but don't knock it till you've tried it. Before going in for the interview, start telling yourself how nervous you are. But *exaggerate*. Don't just tell yourself you're a *little* nervous. Tell yourself you've never been more nervous in your whole life. Tell yourself you're not just nervous, you're frightened. Tell yourself you have to admit you're really terrified. Tell yourself you're a quivering blob of screaming fear. Get some real exaggeration into the whole process. Push it as far as it will go. Tell yourself all the fantastic tragedies that are going to happen because you're paralysed with fear. You're going to be sued for wasting the man's time. The suit's going to drive you into bankruptcy. Your wife's going to leave you now you're a pauper. And so on. If you can find a friend to say all these things to you aloud, so much the better. But do make it a friend. Once you start exaggerating the way you should, a mere acquaintance might start having doubts about your sanity. As you launch into this technique, an amazing psychological mechanism comes into play, and your fears vanish instantly. It's really quite startling when it happens, for it feels as if a blackboard has suddenly been wiped clean. Why it works, nobody quite knows. But it does.

(This is a very useful technique for dealing with other fears, incidentally. One woman I know had built up an irrational fear of the morning post, because it usually contained too many bills. When she learned the technique, she used to come downstairs in the morning muttering aloud about the dire things that awaited her—bills which would have made Paul Getty cringe, lawsuits, threats and the rest. By the time she actually picked up the envelopes, she hadn't a care in the world.)

A third method you might use is the method of *conditioned reflex*. The only drawback with this one is that it requires fairly lengthy preparation. But if you're prepared to invest in the work, you'll develop a tool which will be of use to you for the rest of your life.

You build up the conditioned reflex the same way Pavlov did with his dogs—by association. Every time you're nice and relaxed, warm and happy, mentally repeat a certain word three times. The word itself doesn't matter. You can pick any word that takes your fancy. But if you can't immediately think of one, you're welcome to use the word I usually give to my patients. That word is 'serene'. So every time you're relaxed and happy, repeat the word 'serene' to yourself three times.

For a while, nothing at all will happen. But eventually you'll start to associate the word 'serene' with a feeling of relaxation and happiness. Keep going until the association is firmly established. Then try it the other way round and see what happens.

That's right. Every time you mentally repeat the word 'serene' three times, suddenly you'll start to feel relaxed and happy. You've build up a conditioned reflex. And the more you use it, the stronger it will become. Now you may think that's a pretty useless hint if your interview happens to be tomorrow. And so it is in those circumstances. But you're on the road to personal success now, and tomorrow's interview won't be the last you'll face. So do take time to build the reflex up. You won't regret it.

So now you've prepared yourself for the interview and dealt with any residue of nervousness you may have been feeling. What next? As an exponent of *Power Play*, it's your plan to dominate the interview. Which doesn't mean you have to adopt a bossy or pushy attitude (the fastest way I know to lose a job). What it does mean is that you are planning to direct that interview the way you want it to go, you plan to direct the interview along a route which produces results favourable to yourself. And far from being bossy or pushy, you're going to direct it so subtly that your interviewer won't even know what's happened.

Power Play Domination

Back in the Middle Ages, people believed you could only work magic at certain times. If you didn't know the right time, or accidentally missed it, the spells did as much good as a nursery rhyme. *Power Play* domination is exactly like that. If you don't hit the right time, you're dead. The opportunity comes once, and once only. Miss it, and you're going to have to work very hard and very long to achieve something you could have grabbed in seconds . . . if you ever achieve it at all.

The right time to start *Power Play* domination is the *first available moment*. Exactly how long that 'moment' lasts varies from circumstance to circumstance, but it's best to assume it isn't going to last very long. In other words, start *Power Play* at once. In an interview situation, the interviewer (who's your opponent in *Power Play*) thinks he has control. In a sense, he really does have control to begin with. Let him keep it, or let him consolidate it, or let him gain it and you've lost out.

How, then, do you begin to dominate a situation where, by its very nature, the cards are stacked against you?

The first thing you need to do is *cut your opponent down to size*. Now the funny thing is, a lot of people realize this instinctively. You see the type all the time in business. They go around sneering at other people's work. They make snide comments. They undermine—or try to—just about everything you say. And usually they get nowhere. Because people hate them so much, they're blocked at every turn. But if this is the situation, why am I advocating cutting your opponent down to size? Won't this just mean he'll start to dislike you, and block you from getting the job you're after? Of course it will! But I'm not suggesting you cut your opponent down to size the way most people do it — aggressively and out loud. I'm suggesting you cut your opponent down to size *in your own head*.

In *Power Play*, most games are lost by default. It's not so much that somebody wins, it's more that somebody loses. And the loser is usually you, so long as you have an exaggerated opinion of your opponent. In the interview situation, that sort of exaggerated opinion is almost always there. After all, the interviewer is the man who'll decide whether or not you get the job. That makes him big and powerful before you even see him. If he happens to have a strong personality as well, or a dominant manner, or perhaps just an impressive physical bulk, style of dress or accent, this initial instinct is reinforced.

But, logical or not, instinctive or not, reinforced or not, that notion in your head is wrong. It's wrong because it puts you at a disadvantage in the game of *Power Play*. So, recognizing that the feeling is there, it's vital that you cut the interviewer down to size. Since you've read so far in this book, it won't come as any surprise to learn the way to do this is by visualization.

The minute you walk through the office door and see him sitting there behind his desk, or approaching you to shake hands, you have to make a picture in your mind. And this picture has to remind your unconscious (which controls your attitudes) to see him as he really is, not as he appears to be. So see him playing with his children at the weekend. See him worried over bills. See him hassled by his boss. See him nagged by his little wife. See him exhausted after a hard day.

If you're really desperate, see him sitting on the loo.

Any or all of these mental pictures cut your interviewer down to size. They allow you to deal with him as a fellow human being, rather than the representative of some mysterious, overwhelming power. You might even allow yourself to feel a little sorry for him. After all, he has a difficult job to do in selecting applicants. All the more difficult now that you're here, with your knowledge of *Power Play* techniques.

Where do you go next with *Power Play*? I've already said that you have to dominate the interview. But this most emphatically does *not* mean dominating the interviewer. In fact, it is the essence of *Power Play* that the interviewer feels himself to be on top at all times. Even when he's not. *Especially* when he's not.

You can achieve both your objectives by asking yourself what the interviewer wants to hear. Not what you want to tell him, but what he wants to hear. There's a very real difference between the two. You can reinforce and enlarge your approach by asking yourself what the interviewer wants to *experience*. All these questions are pretty easy to answer. The interviewer wants to experience a pleasant interview, with no undue complications. He wants to experience an end to his problems (finding somebody suitable for the job). He wants to hear that you—yes, you—are the best man for the job. But he wants to hear it so convincingly that there can be no doubt whatsoever in his mind, or anybody else's, about the truth of the statement.

Give him what he wants.

That's the simple *Power Play* secret, so simple that most people miss it. Stop thinking about what you want (the job), or what you want to say. Start thinking about what the interviewer wants, and what he wants to hear. Deliver these goods, and you're home.

Since you've already cut your interviewer down to psychological size and damped out any of your own nervousness, you can automatically begin to treat the interviewer as he really is—a warm, sympathetic human being with a job to do. Once again, how you use *Power Play* principles depends on the circumstances of the situation. But you might begin to dominate the interview by asking him something dear to his own heart—is he having a difficult time sorting out the applicants for the job? This sort of question may surprise him, but it immediately puts you on his own level (and marks you out as a warm, sympathetic human being too). Placing yourself on his level is important. He wants to find the best man for the job, and what better man than somebody on a level with himself?

A question of this type establishes at once who will dominate the interview. Not forceably, not noticeably, but very certainly. From a situation in which you played nervous underdog to his superior efficiency you have moved into a situation of equals. Thus everything else you say will be that much more forceful, that much more effective.

From this situation, you can begin to sell yourself. You already believe in yourself and believe you are the best man available for the job—otherwise you would not have applied in the first place. In these circumstances, it becomes easier and easier to convince your interviewer. Just as nervousness is infectious, so conviction is infectious too—a truism known to every successful salesman.

Don't wait for your interviewer to ask you questions about yourself. He's had to do that a dozen times already with previous applicants and it's only a chore for him. Probe to find out what he feels are the real qualifications of the job, then show him how you fill them. If you start out on the right foot, this probing is easy. Given that you now see yourselves as equals, it does not sound rude or aggressive. The two of you have joined forces to find the solution to the interviewer's problem, to find the best possible man for the job. It just happens that the best possible man is you, that's all, and he'll quickly come to realize it.

Be honest. If your educational background falls short of what he's looking for, tell him so bluntly. Don't dwell on it or try to excuse it, but don't avoid it either. Do, however, explain forcefully why you feel educational attainments are less important in this particular instance than he may have imagined. You already know why, of course, having worked that out for yourself at the time you read the initial ad. Present your own attainments *positively*. In product sales, packaging is known to be important. Few people have yet realized that packaging is just as important in selling yourself. What do I mean by packaging in this context? Let me give you an example.

Two years ago, I listened to a top management consultant

giving a summary of his career to a prospective client. He mentioned the various directorships he'd held, including two posts as managing director. He talked of various top management positions he'd held. Then, since his prospective client was in publishing, he clinched the summary by adding that he had direct experience of the field, having been involved with one of the largest publishers in the British Isles.

The prospective client was instantly interested. 'In what capacity?' he asked.

'Sales and distribution,' the consultant replied. 'With a limited experience of print.' Then he added, 'I don't want to overplay this. The whole thing dates back to my early days, and I wasn't exactly a top executive. Nevertheless, I found the experience gained invaluable.'

The prospective client was duly impressed. So was I, but for a different reason. The consultant's first statements, about his directorships and so on, had been straightforward. But his publishing experience was 'packaged'. He had, in fact, begun his career as the publisher's messenger boy.

This is, of course, an extreme example of packaging, given to show how the most unlikely things can be turned to good account. But packaging yourself effectively can work wonders for your career. Have you worked in more than one country? Then you have *international experience*. Did your last firm have any branches (or a parent company) abroad? Then you worked for a *multi-national corporation*. Do you keep fish for a hobby? You can then describe yourself as *having an interest in marine biology*. Just returned from a trip abroad? Make a throwaway reference to the *rigours of a cosmopolitan existence*. In no case are you lying. In no case are you even exaggerating. You are simply presenting yourself in the best possible light. In a word, packaging. And packaging is a very important aspect of *Power Play*.

Even using *Power Play*, it is impossible to guarantee that you will net every job you try for. After all, the managing director's son may also have put in for the post. But *Power Play* principles can boost your chances to a degree you'd hardly have thought possible. So that, given time, one can virtually guarantee that they will eventually bring you the sort of job you're chasing. And when that day comes, *Power Play* will be even more important to you. Because *Power Play* is the key to a fast climb up the corporate ladder.

11

Climbing The Corporate Ladder

Organizations are peculiar things. You'd think to look at them they were just collections of people working together. But they aren't. For some reason, organizations take on personalities of their own. They start to behave in particular ways.

Sometimes an organization's behaviour pattern will get itself written down and published as a handbook for new employees. In this case, the behaviour pattern will be called something like 'company philosophy' or 'company policy' or, more informally, 'the company way of doing things'. If such a handbook exists in the organization you've joined, it's well worth reading carefully. Not so that you can follow it slavishly, as the company seems to hope. But so that you can use it as a weapon in *Power Play*.

I've yet to meet anyone who did very much for his career by following the company handbook to the letter. When you do that, you're joining the herd. And the nature of herd members is to be anonymous. You won't be noticed as part of the herd. You'll blend delicately into the background and stick there. The man who moves up is the man who stands out from the herd. You stand out by showing imagination, by doing things differently. But doing things differently (even when you're doing them better) means breaking the rules in the handbook.

Why read it at all, then? Why not just go your own way

and build up your reputation willy-nilly? Firstly, because in the early days this is rather a dangerous policy. People don't like to have the boat rocked, so when you start rocking it, as eventually you must, you need to start so gently that it's hardly noticed. Secondly, because the handbook can help you find your feet. It can tell you what the company's up to, give you some idea of how it grew, show you the skeleton of its power structure. All this information is important. It's even more important if you get to know the handbook really well, because you can then quote from it to justify your actions. This may sound a bit odd when, by definition, your actions actually run contrary to the rules in the handbook. But it's all a question of interpretation. There's an old saying that Satan can quote Scriptures to his own advantage. Handbooks are the Scriptures of commercial and industrial organizations. And, while you're destined to show up a great deal better than Old Nick, it can be very useful to refer to them when you're questioned about some course.

You'll find justification from the handbook easy, for a very simple reason. Company principles outlined in handbooks are *general*. They have to be. But your courses of action are *specific*. Given a little patience and a broad interpretation, it's seldom difficult to find a general principle which justifies a specific course of action. And if you fail completely, you can always point out that no progressive company can afford to be completely hidebound by tradition.

Here again you can see *Power Play* principles in action. Your aim is always the gentle manipulation of those around you, particularly your superiors.

If organizations are peculiar things, large organizations are the most peculiar things of all. Many of them engage in policies which a moment's thought would show to be manifestly ludicrous. Take a commonplace form of internal promotion, for instance.

Company structure is generally pyramidical. One man sits at the top (the chairman, or, more usually, the managing director). Below him is a slightly broader layer of directors— the Board level layer. Below that you'll find a layer of top managers. Then a broader layer of middle managers. Then an even broader layer of executives. If the company is in manufacturing, you'll find a similar, secondary pyramid in the factory, with a works manager, possibly responsible to a works director, then assistant managers, factory foremen, charge hands and finally the broad base level of workers.

For many years now, a very popular company policy has been that of internal promotion to fill vacant posts. Superficially, a good case can be made for it. It saves time and money. You don't have to advertise and interview. It guards against costly mistakes (because you know everything about the man who's going to be promoted). It makes for happier staff management relations. It gives employees a strong incentive to work hard.

But it breaks the cardinal rule of a successful company. The rule of efficiency. Let's look carefully at what happens when the internal promotion elevator starts to operate.

A man joins a factory as a machine operator. After a year or so, it becomes obvious that he's an exceptional machine operator. He's careful and conscientious in his work, isn't absent very often, services his machine regularly, gets on well with his mates, and produces fifty per cent more units with his machine than anybody else in the factory. According to the internal promotion policy, he's an obvious target for promotion. A day comes when old Bert, the department foreman, finally retires. Why look further than young Bill, the exceptional machine operator? He knows his job inside out. He's a credit to the company. He's ambitious. He'll 'obviously' make a good foreman.

Nobody stops to consider that a machine operator's job and a foreman's job are two totally different things. Successful machine operation is no indication that young Bill will make a good foreman. It only means that he's made a good machine operator. But he's promoted. And in some cases the promotion pays off. By sheer chance, young Bill turns out to be a grand foreman. In a few years time, he's promoted to the post of general foreman. This move is less risky, since a good department foreman is quite likely to be a good general foreman. So Bill's career is flourishing.

Then the works manager retires, and Bill is promptly slotted in to that post. Once again, nobody stops to think that the job of general foreman (which is concerned with dealing with people and machines) is very different from that of works manager (which may be concerned with economics, sales, broad technical policy and a hundred and one other things).

So Bill moves up to his new post and suddenly, for the first time in his career, finds he's a fish out of water. Little in his previous experience has equipped him for the new job, yet everybody is convinced he's an expert. His standard of work drops alarmingly. It becomes obvious that the company has not only lost an excellent general foreman, but has also gained a poor works manager.

What's to be done? The unfortunate answer is, nothing. Bill can't really be sacked, because of his past record and because that would be admitting a mistake. He can't be moved back down to general foreman again (although that would be the logical thing to do and the move that would ultimately leave Bill happiest) because he would see that as demotion and resent it. So he stays where he is, bumbling along as best he can. He won't be promoted any higher, of course, but he won't be working at anything like peak efficiency in his present post.

This fictional case history illustrates the principle that, in many big companies which practise this form of internal promotion, you're going to find a large number of men who have 'stuck' along the promotion ladder at levels where they are unhappy, inexperienced and inefficient. It's a sobering thought but an interesting thought for an exponent of *Power Play*, as you'll see presently.

*   *   *

In Victorian times, popular morality, encouraged by works of literature, accepted that a man got what he deserved—if not at once, at least ultimately. Observation shows this is seldom true in business. The hard slogger, who puts in hours of unpaid overtime, is conscientious in his work and loyal to the firm, is often passed over when it comes to promotion. By contrast, 'slick operators' frequently move up . . . at least until their limitations are discovered. But there is one principle which does appear to be valid. If businessmen don't always get what they deserve, they certainly seem to get what they *resemble*.

This principle is at the root of much commercial *Power Play*. It dictates obvious things like *Power Play* dress; and less obvious things like *Power Play* mannerisms. It is (I regret to report) the principle of the con man, who has long recognized that if you look like a success, people will treat you like a success.

The essential difference between the con man and the *Power Play* exponent is that the con man is all appearance, with nothing to back it up. The *Power Play* exponent is appearance, plus inner certainty, plus honesty. This latter aspect is vital. Power players are scrupulously honest in their dealings, because honesty is part of the *Power Play* pattern, something which helps ensure a fast run to the top (what company in its right mind is going to promote a crook?).

Let's start now and build up a picture of a power player in a typical organization. Let's find out how he looks and acts, so you can glean the principles of *Power Play* and start to use more of them to your own advantage. We'll start with clothes.

There is a tradition in organization clothes which is so strong it has become almost a uniform. The uniform varies from company to company, or rather from industry to industry. One industry may affect conservative suits, shirts and ties. Another, seeing itself as *avant-garde*, opens up a little, particularly in the case of shirts, which tend to be trendy (I'm purposely not giving actual examples here, because fashions change quite rapidly and what is apt today may well look very dated tomorrow). Artistic organizations, such as design studios, may swing to the other extreme and produce bright individualistic clothes, which nonetheless become the uniform of the organization by the fact that *everybody* has taken to wearing bright, individualistic clothes.

A power player takes note of the 'company uniform' as he takes note of the company manual—not to be guided by it, but to use it.

Clothes are important, and the type of clothes acceptable

to a given company are important. You can't become a top
executive in IBM and turn up in a sloppy sweater and dirty
jeans. But, at the same time, no power player can afford to
adopt the company uniform completely. To do so is to adopt
camouflage. You become indistinguishable from the
background. You become part of the herd. Which acts like a
landslide on the road to success.

So you can't afford to look like the herd and you can't
afford to be radically different. Where does that leave you?
Here's the guiding *Power Play* principle:

The power player dresses to look independent. Not
outlandish, not freaky, not eccentric, not colourful, not
flamboyant, but *independent*.

Success Clothing

How does this work out in practise? Suppose, for example,
the company's 'executive uniform' (the unwritten, voluntary
style in which most of the executives dress) is a dark suit of
modern cut worn with a broad-striped shirt and dark tie. The
power player need not deviate from this standard one iota.
But he will make absolutely sure everything he wears is a cut
or two above the average—a noticeable cut or two above the
average. His shoes may be black, like the rest . . . but they're
hand-made, Italian shoes. His suit may be dark, like the rest
. . . but it's a tailored three-piece, while the rest are off the
peg. His shirt may be styled like the rest . . . but the maker's
lable marks it out as several degrees better. Put all this
together and you have success clothing. Clothing which sits
better, looks better and seems a good deal more expensive.
The power player carries this policy through to accessories.
He'll be the first man in the building with a quartz crystal
watch. The best quartz crystal watch. And the cuff-links,
while discrete, are 18 carat gold. He looks, in short, as if he
were dressed rather better than he should be able to afford.
He looks like a man with some independent means.

But if you're not, in fact, a man of independent means,
isn't this a fast route to bankruptcy? Oddly enough, the
answer is no. Far too many men make far too many
assumptions. And the assumptions block useful courses of
action. They're exactly like imaginary limitations in this
respect.

There's an assumption that quality tailoring is expensive. It isn't. It may require a capital outlay slightly above average, but it lasts longer. What you lose on the swings, you gain on the roundabouts. Tiny gold cuff-links, which look tasteful, will often come less expensive than more flamboyant items in less precious metal, which simply succeed in looking flash. And so on.

It pays to shop around. It pays to use discrimination. It pays to use imagination. All these things can save you money, while leaving you well-dressed. And today's credit-oriented society means that, in most cases, you won't even have to lay out capital if you don't want to.

While independence of dress is important to the power player, independence of manner is even more so. Which isn't to say the successful power player is domineering and aggressive. On the contrary, he tends to be friendly and relaxed. He seldom raises his voice, because he seldom has to. He is aware of granny's ancient maxim that you catch more flies with honey than with vinegar. But above all, he is aware of body language and its subtle clues of dominance.

Pecking Order

The 'pecking order' is a biological phenomenon originally discovered in the lives of barnyard hens—hence its odd name. Scientific observers discovered that hens had a rigidly structured society, layered in levels of dominance. Those hens which lived within the bottom social layer might be freely pecked by every other hen in the flock, but did not peck back. Hens in the next layer up could peck at hens in the layer below, but could not peck hens in the social strata above them. And so on, until you reach the hen who could peck everybody, but was never pecked in return. Wider studies showed that the pecking order was not confined to hens. Layers of dominance were observed in a number of animal societies, from tribes of apes to herds of elk. There was always a top banana who had freedom of action and choice of mates, followed by lesser bananas of dwindling importance, who had less and less power, less and less authority, the further down the social ladder they were placed.

The parallels between these findings and human society, particularly as it manifests in commercial organizations, are pretty obvious. A managing director can bawl out a department manager, but the department manager can't bawl back. At the same time, the department manager is free to tick off those under him in the administrative ladder.

In animal societies, the actual order of dominance is generally established on the basis of physical strength. The dominant bull ape literally fights his way to the top. But the order is maintained by something a lot more subtle. While the supremo is occasionally challenged to physical combat, supremacy fights are comparatively rare. In the day-to-day life of the tribe, the social stratification is maintained by a whole series of *signals*. These signals, so far as we can determine, are delivered and received at an unconscious level. But they tell very clearly who's boss and who's not.

Using Body Language

It is a principle of *Power Play* that a similar signal system exists in the world of business. You've probably noticed it in operation yourself, without being altogether aware of what was going on. You might, for example, be sitting in the foyer of a large hotel when a man walks in and, without apparent effort, instantly commands the attention of the staff. The same thing happens in restaurants. Some men can catch the waiter's eye with ease. Others signal wildly without result. In a group, one man is automatically presented with the bill because he looks, somehow, as if he was in charge. In certain circumstances it's possible to analyse logically why these things happen. The hotel visitor might be known to the staff as a heavy tipper. The man 'in charge of the group' might be older than his colleagues. But time after time, logical criteria just don't apply. An individual stands out because he stands out. There doesn't seem to be any real reason for it.

But there is a reason. Dominant individuals naturally send out a whole host of unconscious signals, which are instantly (and equally unconsciously) picked up by those around them. These signals do not depend exclusively on wealth, or dress, or accent—although wealth, dress and accent often act as signals in themselves. They depend, in the main, on something called *body language*.

Body language is something else that's come in for a fair amount of scientific attention lately. It makes a fascinating study, for we all use it, whether we know it or not. Notice people sitting chatting at a party. Notice the way they cross their legs. In fact, legs are crossed and bodies slightly turned towards the focus of attention. These same body attitudes will tend to cut a bore out of a gathering—even when people are politely pretending to listen to him.

Body language can send out all sorts of signals. A man can signal aggression simply by the way he stands—a point taken up and grossly exaggerated in many Western films. A girl can signal acceptance of masculine attention by the way she sits— and even signal in advance how far she wants that attention to go!

But, fascinating though all this is, it takes us away from the main use of body language in *Power Play*. For the power player is almost exclusively interested in the body language of dominance. And the reason for this is another power play principle. While body language signals are usually unconscious, they can be learned and used consciously by a power player.

A prime essential of the dominant stance is upright posture. Body language signals have very primitive roots, as we've noted from animal studies. They are symbolic reflections of dominance based on physical violence. When you are losing a fight, there is a very natural tendency to bend over, crouch down, cover up vital organs. Only when you're winning can you afford to stand upright.

The upright stance has another basis, again rooted in the concept of physical dominance. When it comes to a fight, the bigger animal usually wins. Many creatures are equipped with biological mechanisms which allow them to appear bigger than they actually are in confrontation situations. A cat's fur will stand on end. Certain birds puff up their feathers. And so on. In man, the upright stance fulfils this same function. Models are advised to 'walk tall'. It gives them that aristocratic (dominant) look so prized by fasion designers.

Thus the power player cultivates an upright posture. But not the stiff, pouter-pigeon look of a company sergeant major. He is upright, but relaxed. He is especially upright and relaxed in the company of his business superiors.

A second essential of the dominant stance is the steady gaze. This one is a lot more difficult to cultivate than upright posture, for reasons which will soon become clear. But it is almost as important as posture, and in certain circumstances can be even more so. Stare at your pet dog or cat. After a moment it will look away. It may even show a measure of discomfort. The animal is reacting to the clearly signalled dominance of the human being, admitting its own inferiority in the natural order of things.

Unfortunately, staring directly at your fellow humans is not enough. All it really does is get you a reputation for rudeness or eccentricity. A steady gaze is something else again. It expresses, above all, a willingness to look someone in the eye, calmly and confidently. The power player never engages in 'staring matches', which are a childish form of the dominance game and should have been outgrown at puberty. But he will never avoid another man's eye, either. He also knows that to watch a person's mouth when they are talking denotes interest. Looking away can be made to denote thoughtfulness. And the right kind of eye contact can denote cynicism, or amusement. The power player uses his eyes to keep control of a situation.

A third essential in the body language of *Power Play* is deliberate movements. Only underlings scurry. The dominant man tends to move not slowly, but quite deliberately. He has the necessary time and he takes it. He can move fast when he wants to, but never seems quite to hurry.

The picture I've built up in its three essentials clearly illustrates the difference between 'dominant' and 'domineering'. The dominant man smiles a lot, pays attention to the needs of those under him. He's polite to waiters and servants. He seems very human. But his overriding characteristic is dominance. His upright stance, confident gaze, deliberate movements and relaxed posture all mark him out as a man in control. He is a man of substance, a man of independent judgement. The signals are there for all (unconsciously) to see.

By now, you may have started to notice how the principles

of *Power Play* blend into one another. Although this book has been divided into two sections, it is a division of convenience. Preparing for success (the initial section) is as much a part of *Power Play* as any of the principles outlined in the present section. If the dominant stance requires confidence and relaxation, then the preparatory exercises designed to build confidence and relaxation are obviously a part of the technique of the dominant stance. And the fact that this preparation was done in advance turns out to be extremely important, because the establishment of dominance is best done early. In fact, it is best done at first meeting, because first impressions can lay the foundations for many future reactions. Unless you establish dominance early, you are going to have to fight for it hard at a later date.

People are both conservative and lazy by nature. If, on first acquaintance, they have marked you down as a low-dominance individual, it takes a great deal to make them change their minds later. And the power player has better things to do than work for something which could have been picked up for nothing at the right time.

He has, for example, to learn about the power of territory.

12

The Power of Territory

Robert Ardrey wrote a fine book called *The Territorial Imperative*. It's required reading for every *Power Play* operative. It's required reading even though it doesn't deal with business, or dominance, or even, in the main, with human beings. It's required reading because it suggests another weapon for the power player's armoury.

The Territorial Imperative is an accurate, highly readable popularization of scientific investigation into a peculiarity of animal behaviour associated with the idea of territory. I'm no Robert Ardrey, but I'll try to give you an idea of the findings. Roughly speaking, what's happened is this:

Naturalists now divide animal species into territorial and non-territorial species. It's the territorial species that are of interest to us at the present moment. Members of a territorial species associate themselves, for some reason, with a particular bit of land. There's an area of the jungle, or the plain, which they just naturally consider to be theirs. This area has very clear-cut boundaries, which are recognized instinctively by every member of the tribe or herd. The deeper inside its own territory a territorial animal happens to be, the happier it is. When it starts to move out towards the boundaries, it gets wary. If, for any reason, it has to *cross* the boundary, it gets downright nervous.

So far this is fair enough, but there's a lot more to territory than meets the eye. To illustrate the point and make the description easier, let's assume we're dealing with a tribe of African baboons. The baboon is a territorial species, so the tribe has a clearly defined district which it considers its own. The baboons hunt within that district, mate within that district. The females, the old baboons and the weak or ill baboons will tend to stick to the heartland of the territory because they feel safer there. Next door to our baboon tribe is another baboon tribe, which also has a territory. The boundary line between the two territories is a tiny, shallow stream. Every so often, these two tribes of baboons have a baboon hassle. They don't actually go to war, but members of the tribes, with the big males in the vanguard, have a sort of border confrontation. This usually comes about when too many tribal hunters have been operating near the boundary. Members of the other tribe, seeing their neighbours approaching the boundary, seem to fear an invasion of their own territory and send for reinforcements. When the reinforcements arrive, the hunters on the other side figure an invasion of *their* territory is on the cards, so they send word back to their own colleagues. Before you know it, both tribes are up their in strength at the border, shouting insults across the stream, making rude baboon gestures, showing off their muscles and occasionally throwing rocks.

But the funny thing is, the tribes don't cross the stream. Occasionally, when the excitement's running very high, a young male with more aggro than sense might make a quick dash over the boundary, but he won't stay very long. It's all sound and fury, and very little fisticuffs. Eventually, everybody gets tired of the show and moves back stiffly to the heartland. While it's all been a bit of an anti-climax after the initial excitement, it does illustrate one important point. Territory has to be *defended*.

There are times when an invasion actually does take place. It's usually accidental, but it's an invasion for all that. When food gets scarce, a tribe will range wider and wider within its own territory. Eventually, it may cross over a boundary without noticing. The tribe will stay in the neighbouring territory until discovered. Which is when another unexpected situation arises. The tribe might be discovered by just a few prowling hunters from the other tribe which actually owns the territory. You might have forty invading baboons and only nine or ten home team baboons. And you might think with odds like that in their favour, the invaders could afford to thumb their noses and sit tight.

But it doesn't happen. Those few home baboons fling themselves savagely on the invaders and, after a bit of a scrap, the invaders race back towards the border screaming their heads off. Typically, the home baboons will chase them right up to the boundary, then stop, wait around for a time, then go home to the heartland. Which illustrates another point. You fight better on your own territory. Territory seems to give added strength and power.

All this is very interesting, but it isn't very useful unless we have an answer to the $64,000 question. Is Man a territorial species?

The scientists are divided, but it certainly seems like it. When Russia invaded Finland before the Second World War, it looked as if that little Scandinavian country wouldn't have a prayer. But the Finnish army was fighting on its home territory, and the result was a massive Russian embarrassment. Right from its inception, the State of Israel showed itself more than able to withstand concerted attacks from its Arab neighbours. South Africa has for years been under economic seige because of its apartheid policies, and has grown internally strong as a result.

Of course, territory is not a magic superweapon. Given enough force, any territory can be successfully invaded and overrun. But territory gives a definite edge. When you fill in your football pools, you receive more points for an away win than a home win. Away wins are harder to forecast because, statistically, any team tends to play better on its home ground.

Personal Space and Living Space

The power player assumes that mankind is a territorial species. More to the point, he accepts individual men as territorial animals. And this gives him another level to control them. In the world of business, as in many other spheres of human activity, there are two kinds of territory. To differentiate between them, I propose to call one *personal space* and the other *living space*.

Personal space is that small area surrounding your body beyond which you prefer most people not to approach. Its actual size and sensitivity varies from person to person. You can chart the boundaries of personal space by a very simple experiment. Ask a friend to stand in the middle of a room. Walk very slowly towards him. Have him call 'Stop' the instant your approach begins to make him feel uncomfortable. When he does so, you've discovered the outer boundary of his personal space. Psychiatrists in the United States carried out a series of experiments with psychopaths, and found they were so sensitive to an invasion of their personal space that they often reacted with violence when somebody crossed that invisible barrier. Not everybody is as bad as this, of course, but to most people personal space is very important indeed. You see an unconscious recognition of the fact in crowded buses and tube trains. Here personal space is violated by the minute. But people standing shoulder to shoulder draw themselves in and avoid eye contact, as if to apologize for the necessary invasion.

Living space, as I define it, is something different. Living space is home—living space in the sense of the space you can live in most comfortably. It can literally be your own home. Or it can be your office. Or it can be a favourite armchair. There are little areas on the surface of this globe where you, as an individual, are more comfortable, more secure than others. It's not exactly your territory, because that's a tribal term and almost certainly refers to the land you live in. So I'm calling it living space to differentiate. It's personal territory, I suppose, as opposed to tribal or species territory.

So what's all this got to do with *Power Play?* Quite a lot, as it happens. Both personal space and living space have their psychological rules, and a knowledge of them puts the power player ahead of the field. Let me give you an example of how strong territorial rules can be. Irrational, illogical, sometimes silly, but immensely strong. This is something you've probably experienced, without really knowing what was going on.

You've gone to visit a close friend. You arrive at his house, possibly after a long journey, and you find he's out. The house is deserted. In those circumstances, can you think of anything more logical, more reasonable than slipping round the back to see if a window's been left open, then climbing inside to wait for your friend in warmth and comfort? You know if he was there he would welcome you in. You know he would never think of objecting if he came back to find you in residence. You know he would hate to feel you'd come all that way to see him and had to turn and go home again. So it's reasonable to break in — right?

It may be reasonable, but it's very uncomfortable. You walk round the back feeling like a criminal. There's a tendency to jumpiness, to look over your shoulder. If you do break in, you sit in the chair uneasily, stiffly. You can't relax. You don't quite know what to do next. Sudden sounds make you jump. The whole empty house seems to glower at you.

You're experiencing the power of territory.

In the business context, you can turn this power to good account. It's a well known psychological ploy to call an underling into your office rather than going to his. It establishes status and keeps you in control. But the ploy is often used unconsciously. The boss never thinks of strolling down to somebody else's office. He just lifts the 'phone and tells them to stroll on down to his. Which is all very fine, except that the essence of *Power Play* is conscious manipulation, not instinctive reaction.

When the power player wants to talk to someone, he refuses to trust his instincts about where the talk should take place. He analyses the situation consciously. This is particularly important when he's talking to someone at his own level in the organization. His instinct might tell him that he should go to John's office. His analysis will tell him that this is an admission of John's natural superiority, even though, theoretically, they're on a par. In another case, the power player might want to talk to somebody lower down the business ladder. His instinct tells him to call the underling to his office. But analysis might well show it would be better for the power player to do the walking. The simple gesture can mark him out as a decent superior, someone who wasn't afraid to be one of the boys. It might allow him to make the underling more relaxed. And so on. The power player shows dominance when it is useful to him, not when it is instinctive to him.

Various factors have to be carefully weighed up and balanced. If, for instance, you only want to check some figures or hand in a memo, it will usually pay the power player to do the walking. But if it's an important confrontration situation, nature dictates you'll do better within your own living space—in this case, your office. Thus you should make every attempt to see that's where the confrontation takes place.

But if that simply isn't possible, you can still use your knowledge of personal space to swing the psychological factors in your direction. Here's an experiment you can try next time you're at a two-man business lunch. It will give you the feel of manipulating personal space to your advantage. It's designed, quite simply, to make your companion feel uncomfortable and on edge, without his quite realizing why. And though it's purely in the nature of an experiment, you can see how the technique *might* be used to take the edge off a business opponent during contract negotiations.

The setting for the experiment is this. You're in a restaurant with Joe, your business colleague. You're sitting facing one another across a smallish table. There's a bottle of wine on the table (a blessing on expense accounts!), the food's usually good and the restaurant has a pleasant atmosphere. You're both very relaxed to begin with. What neither of you can see is a line which divides your table in half. You can't see it, but it's there all right, as real as if you'd drawn it carefully with chalk. On one side of the line is Joe's personal space. On the other side is yours.

When you use the salt, instead of placing it on the line (i.e. in the middle) afterwards, you place it casually on Joe's side. This is perfectly acceptable—even polite—if you happen to be using the salt first. But in this case, I'd like to assume Joe has already used it. You take up the pepper shaker, which Joe has already used. You set that down again inside his personal space. You don't have to be obvious or exaggerated—an inch or two over that invisible line will do. There's a small vase of fresh flowers on the table. You fiddle nervously with them, then move them so you can talk to Joe better. You move them into his personal space. You take a drink of wine and set your glass casually down just beyond the invisible line, in Joe's personal space.

Consciously, Joe won't realize you're mounting an invasion. It won't strike him (unless he's a power player too) that you're expanding your personal space at the expense of his. But his unconscious will know all right. And Joe will grow progressively more uncomfortable, irritated, perhaps even downright angry.

An Office Confrontation

In an office confrontation, you can use a modification of this technique in order to get the upper hand, to make your business opponent lose his cool, to take the edge off his feeling of control. Bear in mind we're examining a confrontation which takes place in your opponent's office, so the edge is with him to begin with. He's fighting on his own territory and is all the stronger because of it.

Almost certainly he'll greet you from behind his desk. His seat is personal space and the desk itself is at once a psychological barrier and a symbol of his superiority. There'll be a chair directly opposite his across the desk. You're expected to sit in it. Really tough opponents sit with the light behind them, a crude, but highly effective form of psychological domination reputedly widely used by policemen administering the third degree. But though the cards are stacked against you, as a power player you can deal with the situation's psychological undertones quite simply. Move the chair round beside him. This is a gross invasion of his personal space, cunningly disguised as an act of intimacy and friendship. It is beautiful in its simplicity, and often quite devastating in its results. The edge is no longer with your opponent.

You may, of course, prefer to take the edge off in other ways. Really aggressive power players will lean across a desk, either standing or from the sitting position, depending on the level of dominance they want to project. Others might produce a single copy of a report for discussion and use it as an excuse to get round the desk to their opponent. But whatever method is chosen, the principle remains the same.

You are mounting an invasion of territory in such a way that your opponent cannot take open steps to repulse it. As a result, he becomes uncomfortable and loses the psychological edge given him by his living space.

Another interesting use of territorial invasion is cutting your opponent's lines of communication.

Modern offices are suprisingly mechanized. When the man behind the desk wants to talk to somebody in the building, or outside, he reaches for the intercom or 'phone. Most offices combine the two functions in a single instrument—a 'phone with buttons which give an outside line and buttons which connect direct to other offices. For any businessman at his desk, this instrument is his prime line of communication. Experience has taught him its importance. He uses it all the time. And because of this use, it has taken on an emotional significance. But the emotional significance remains unconscious.

A secondary line of communication is, unexpectedly, his dictaphone. Today, the larger desk-top models have generally been replaced by small, portable machines. These, too, have an emotional significance for the man who uses them habitually. And here, too, the significance is unconscious.

A power player cuts an opponent's lines of communication by moving one, or both of these machines out of his reach. For preference, he will move the 'phone. This can be done relatively smoothly with a little thought. Perhaps papers have to be spread out on the desk. The 'phone is moved to 'make room'. The experienced power player will take it off the desk altogether and leave it on the floor on the opposite side of the desk from his opponent. Even taking the 'phone off the hook ('We don't want to be disturbed by incoming calls, do we?') can be a very effective cutting of the communication line.

The result is an opponent whose inner sense of security has been sliced down a little. Once again, the edge has been taken off. Once again, the psychological card-stacking against the power player has been counteracted.

A power player's knowledge of personal space can be useful in circumstances other than confrontation. It's a fact of life that those who may invade our personal space with impunity are intimates. This is most clearly illustrated in romantic situations. Lovers cling together, all considerations of personal space gone by the board. Invasion is positively welcomed and encouraged. But there are various degrees of intimacy, and these are clearly reflected by the degree of personal space habitually allowed between the intimates.

In business, as in many human activities, knowledge is power. And knowledge of the state of business relationships can be very useful indeed. It allows the power player to judge the real hierarchy in an organization, as opposed to the apparent one. He can judge the boss's current favourite, or recognize which of the executives the marketing manager really likes, simply by observing the degree of personal space allowed when they are talking together. An open breach of personal space, such as a hand on the arm or shoulder, is a clear signal that a high degree of trust and intimacy exists, whatever the positions of the men involved.

*   *   *

The use of *Power Play* is, of course, cumulative. The dominant stance is useless unless you have first learned how to relax, and taken time to develop your own self-confidence through visualization. Tricks like invasion of personal space, or cutting the lines of communication, are useless unless you have established the power player personality which can carry them out smoothly. Knowledge of your colleague's hierarchical positions is little more than a curio unless you can take advantage of it. But if you have faithfully followed the development of the power player personality in the sequence outlined in this book, you'll quickly find that one thing leads naturally on to another.

Within this natural progression, any knowledge of what makes people tick is very useful, and even the best book in the world can't tell you everything there is to know about human nature. In fact, much of the most useful knowledge of human nature isn't based on textbook study at all. It's based on direct observation. As a developing power player, observation should be one of your most consistent functions. You should constantly ask yourself why people act the way they do, constantly try to predict how they would react in certain circumstances. And if the circumstances actually arise, you should observe how they do in fact react, and see how it equates with your prediction.

The learning process never stops. And since you're now well on the way to becoming a fully-fledged power player, you might like to try a simple test to see how much you've learned so far—both from this book and from simple direct observation.

Before you try the test, I want to give you one important piece of information. It may sound startling to you, but it's true for all that. The information is that the vast majority of your business colleagues are harbouring a guilty secret.

The test (which you should try before reading the next chapter, which gives the answer) is for you to decide what that guilty secret might be.

13

The Secret Of The Guilty Secret

The test was a lot easier than you imagine. You already knew the answer. You'd been told it in Part One of this book.

Remember the chapter about self-image? Remember how we saw what gives you those feelings of inadequacy, those feelings of inferiority, of insecurity? In all probability, we were talking openly for the first time about something you usually keep well hidden.

Think back on it. Think back to before the time you started your *Power Play* visualization exercises. Remember how much energy you used hiding the things you thought made you inferior? What was it then? Maybe something silly, like a fear of thunderstorms. You never mentioned it to anybody, because you thought it would make you look childish. Maybe it was something deeper, like the fact that you aren't attractive to the opposite sex. But you never admitted that to anybody. Or maybe you knew you couldn't handle your job efficiently—a business secret you'd never share with anybody except perhaps your psychiatrist or your wife.

A whole host of possible secrets, but they all come down to one secret. This is the secret of your own inferiority. And you worried so much about that guilty secret that it never occurred to you that those around you had a guilty secret too. The secret of *their* own inferiority.

That's right. Your colleague's guilty secret is exactly the

same secret you used to have before you took up *Power Play*. The hidden knowledge of their own supposed inferiority. The buried recognition of their own shortcomings. It's a secret that's hung around humanity for a long, long time now. It's literally as old as sin, because a sense of sinning springs directly from this feeling of inferiority.

Most people go to great pains to conceal it. It's what makes bullies and boasters, dictators and wife-beaters. All putting up brave, brash fronts to hide that guilty secret from the world. But the more they try to hide it, the more potent the secret becomes. That's a strange thing, but something well borne out by the findings of modern psychology. Secrets grow in darkness. Keep a thing well hidden in your mind, and before you know it your whole life is practically devoted to keeping it hidden. And the secret's strongest of all if you manage to keep it hidden from yourself.

The reverse is equally true. Once you let the secret out into the open, it withers and dies. Its power discharges. That's one of the principles of psycho-analysis, incidentally. Only it doesn't work so well, because the secret isn't really let out into the open. It's simply shared with the analyst, who's bound by professional etiquette to keep it secret too. But though the reverse is true, very few people ever find the courage to let out their guilty secret. If anything, they try to bury it deeper. Should they suspect someone has discovered it, or is coming close to discovering it, they grow very uncomfortable indeed.

The power player knows the secret of the guilty secret. He knows that almost everyone around him, no matter how secure they seem, no matter what power they wield, is secretly plagued by deeply-buried feelings of inferiority.

How does the power player put this knowledge to use?

First of all, he puts it to use inside himself. As you know by now, there are two basic aspects of *Power Play*—personal change and growth on the one hand, manipulation of external circumstances and people on the other. The power player is seldom obvious, and his first use of the secret of the guilty secret is subtle.

Personal change comes slowly. It's like an oak tree growing from an acorn. You can water the plant well, tend it with loving care, fertilize it regularly, protect it from damage, but there are still limits to how fast you can make it grow.

Power Play visualizations act as a sort of forcing house to personal change. But even using them, the full change comes slowly. The new power player may be able to handle specific situations easily enough, using his knowledge and techniques. But there are still times when the old feelings of inferiority come creeping back. He can usually control them, of course, but he still looks forward to the day when he can flatten them altogether.

His knowledge of the guilty secret is something which will hasten that day. When a power player feels low, he first tells himself something. He reminds himself *he's now an adult*. In his mind he dwells on childhood scenes. He visualizes the world as it was when he was young. He sees himself surrounded by giants, by men of almost limitless power and authority. And he reminds himself he has now become one of those giants.

When the going is rough, he asks himself what bad things can possibly happen to him. He is now an adult, with power and control. He is now one of the mighty giants he knew as a child. Nothing bad can possibly happen to him. And, having reminded himself of his adult status, he then contrasts himself with his colleagues. On the surface, the contrast shows him up both well and badly. On the surface, some of his colleagues appear more successful, more powerful, more authoritative. Then the power player reminds himself of their guilty secret. Suddenly, the situation changes. He sees them for what they really are—unsure, frightened human beings with little hope of change.

He sees himself for what he really is: a power player who has his own destiny within his own grasp, a man with the potential to control his environment and future because he has the potential to control himself. The reminder serves its purpose. The contrasts cease to be a mixture of good and bad, and become simply good. In real terms, the power is vested in the other members of that crowd.

This is not the only use of the secret of the guilty secret. And, once again, the power player is subtle in his use of it.

Using the 'Guilty Secret' Positively

A lesser man who learns the secret might be tempted to use it directly against his colleagues. To drop hints, make references, persuade his colleagues he knows the truth and thus leave them so uncomfortable that they work with less efficiency, that they become afraid of him. But the power player will have none of this. He is interested in the road to success, and if the road was obvious, many more men would travel it.

The power player uses the secret of the guilty secret to *help* his colleagues. He uses it to make them more secure. He uses it to reassure them. He uses it to increase their measure of happiness. And in the process, the power player achieves two things. He builds a reputation and he develops empathy.

The reputation he builds is an enviable one. For it's the reputation of a 'good guy'. Someone sympathetic and understanding. Someone who appreciates a person's difficulties. Someone who knows what makes people tick. Someone with insight. Someone who can be trusted. It's a success reputation. Someone who can be trusted on a personal level can obviously be trusted with greater responsibility. Someone who has insight on a personal level will obviously show insight into business problems. Someone who understands what makes people tick should obviously be groomed for management. All this, plus the fact that the power player is making himself widely liked. And though, theoretically, personal likes and dislikes should play little part in business, the fact is that they do.

The development of empathy is closely associated with the projection of a 'good guy' personality. The dictionary definition of empathy is the ability to feel what others are feeling. It develops quickly when a power player recognizes that many of his colleagues' actions spring from their deep-rooted sense of insecurity. With this knowledge he is able to cope with them better, to sympathize with their problems. People sense empathy as a thirsty horse senses water. This leads to their entrusting the power player with confidences, and to a ready acceptance of his advice in a variety of situations. As a result, he can quickly build up a level of authority and prestige far beyond his actual position with the organization. It's seldom long before this reality is recognized in the form of promotion. It is a *power play* maxim that empathy and upward mobility go hand in hand.

*   *   *

In business, you can't go higher than the Boardroom. Even if you make chairman or managing director, your field of *Power Play* operations is still the Boardroom. Fortunately it's an environment where the experienced power player comes into his own.

There's a reason for this. Despite the fictionalized picture of captains of industry logically charting the troubled waters of commerce, Boardrooms are in fact hothouses of personality interaction. The man who can handle his fellow men is the man who is most successful at Board level. And nobody handles his fellow men better than a good power player.

Let me give you an example of how things might work out in your own case. You've been with the company a few years. You've used the principles of *Power Play* to establish yourself as obvious Boardroom material. You know more about the key men in your organization than many of them know about themselves. You've done your job honestly and conscientiously, so that your past record is sound. One afternoon, the managing director invites you out to lunch. It's a casual enough invitation, but the restaurant he's chosen is a cut or two above the type of place usually frequented by the boys. As a power player, you see this as a signal. Something's up. And whatever it is looks promising.

You're driven to the restaurant in the MD's car. The talk on route is at a pretty superficial level. Current developments on the latest contract. Vague plans for future expansion. The staffing problem in the Maintenance Department. As a power player, you're feeling relaxed and confident. You're not particularly worried about what the invitation's all about, because, whatever it is, you know you can handle it. If anything, you're more concerned about the standard of the food.

You arrive at the restaurant and are shown to a quiet table

by the window. Without fuss, you make sure the managing director gets the best seat, with lots of personal space. No crowding here—you want him relaxed. The waiter brings the menu and you both study it. As a power player you will automatically ask his opinion on the restaurant's standards with a particularly exotic dish. You explain that you enjoy Siberian cuisine (or whatever style the dish belongs to) but have found that few Western cooks can handle it effectively. Accept his advice without question. In one easy manoeuvre, you've shown yourself *au fait* with the mysteries of the international kitchen and flattered him by giving him credit for even greater knowledge than your own. You're treating him casually as an equal, but suggesting subtly that in some respects you might even be his superior.

The managing director may well ask you to choose the wine. By now you'll have established something of a reputation as a wine connoisseur. You've established it by the simple expedient of studying French wines. And you've studied them the most efficient way. You first learned the difference between Bordeaux and Burgundy. The former is usually lighter, the latter usually more full-bodied. You can tell the difference between the two by the shape of the bottle (Bordeaux has the square shouldered bottle. Burgundy bottles have sloping shoulders and look plumper). You know that heavily flavoured dishes require a heavily flavoured wine and vice versa, so you know when to zero in on Burgundy and when to call for Bordeaux. You know a really lightly flavoured dish—like fish or some of the whiter meats—requires the even lighter flavour of white wine. You know the law of contrasts. A dry wine tastes positively bitter with a dessert. What's needed here is the cloying sweetness of a good Sauterne. But sweet wine—or even medium sweet wine—with the remainder of the meal interferes appreciably with the flavour of the food. And, of course, an aperitif must always be dry—preferably very dry—because the sugar content of a sweet wine actively turns down the body's appetite control and ruins the enjoyment of the meal.

You've learned the secret of the 'good years'. Nothing really mysterious about them, despite the snobbery and mystique which surrounds them. They're simply those years when there was a fine summer on the Continent. The amount of sunshine controls the quality of the grape, and the quality of the grape controls the quality of the wine. And, having learned the basics, you've learned the characteristics of a few good chateaux. So you can find your way through a wine list without any real trouble. Like good power players everywhere, you're honest. You never overstate your knowledge, although you do perhaps package it well. When someone comments on your reputation as a wine expert, you shrug and tell them you know perhaps a little about French wines, but German and Italian wines are a complete mystery to you. Your manner suggests that when you know about the best, the rest can take care of itself. (If your managing director happens to be German or Italian, ask him to teach you about the great wines of his country.)

So, having been asked to chose the wine, you do so with confidence. When the waiter pours a little for you to taste, you do not in fact taste it at all. You sniff it. Ostensibly you accept that a good restaurant will never serve you a bottle of poor wine. You sniff only to ensure no cork has reached the liquid. If the wine has gone off—as sometimes happens even in the best of cellars—your nose will tell you quickly enough.

And so a pleasant meal begins. You eat it with enjoyment, letting your managing director set the conversational pace. When the cigars arrive, you're careful to remove the band before smoking yours. You may even indulge yourself in a little minor *Power Play* with the story of the cigar band and why it has to be removed.

In more elegant days, you comment lightly, gentlemen habitually wore white gloves which were badly stained by cigar smoke. So the cigar makers introduced cigar bands to protect the gloves. But the *real* gentlemen were not prepared to admit they could not afford new gloves when the old ones were stained. Thus they habitually removed the band before smoking. The gesture eventually became the mark of the real gentleman. And if your managing director didn't remove the band before he heard that engaging bit of nonsense, he certainly will afterwards.

In this relaxed and pleasant atmosphere, the managing director finally gets to the point. You are invited to join the

Board. He sits back smugly to watch your reaction. So do you, because this is an important point in your career. You must react positively and with pleasure. It is, after all, an honour to be asked into the Boardroom. But don't over-react. Effusiveness is totally out of character for a power player. Accept the invitation with warmth and pleasure. Then immediately ask if your new directorship includes an option on shares.

Both the question and the timing are vital. Most employees are so hypnotized by the very idea of a directorship that they forget where the real power in any company lies. But the power player is always aware that it lies with the shareholders. And even a small investment is better than none.

The timing is important because of your managing director's mood. It may be that a share option was part of the deal and he merely neglected to mention it. If so, he'll be happy you've reminded him. Even if it was not, he'll have a difficult job refusing to consider your request in the circumstances. At very worst, you'll have marked yourself out as a shrewd businessman. Even if the request is turned down at this stage, keep making it in the months ahead. Shareholding is vital. Sooner or later, the power player has to get it.

Whatever happens, don't forget to thank him for the lunch (you might even casually use his first name). As you leave the restaurant, you might consider you have something very interesting to look forward to.

Your first Board meeting.

As a power player, that's going to be a challenge and a pleasure.

14

Staying On Top

There's an old show business saying: 'Be nice to the people you meet on the way to the top. Because you'll have to meet them again on the way back down.'

The power player has, in fact, 'been nice' to the people he met on the way to the top. But when he reaches his goal he aims to stay right where he is. Like almost everything else in *Power Play*, his first step in his direction is an inward step, a visualization exercise. To be precise, a visualization of stability. The signal is hoisted to the unconscious: *Here I am and here I want to stay*.

By now, you should be able to construct the relevant pictures quite easily for yourself. Visualize yourself coping efficiently and effectively with your work. See yourself living the sort of life you want to lead. With your knowledge and experience of *Power Play*, staying at the top should present no real difficulties. But there are one or two simple techniques which you may find useful, especially at first, before you become the grand old man of the firm whose judgment is universally respected and whose word is law.

Let's take a quick look at your first Board meeting and how to handle it. The technique is one you can use anytime it's necessary. It's especially useful at conferences where you wish to establish a dominant status without appearing aggressive.

As you walk into your first Board meeting, you'll be very

much the centre of attention, simply because it is your first. Your fellow directors will welcome you warmly, of course, but behind the smiles they'll be wondering how you'll handle yourself, wondering if you'll show as much promise in your new status as you did before you became a director. Nobody will expect you to do very much at your first meeting. Most newcomers sit tight and try to learn the ropes. That's a traditional approach and not such a bad approach at that. Too much early enthusiasm and too little experience have often combined to help a man make a fool of himself.

The meeting starts, and for a while it looks as though you've decided on the traditional route. You sit there, alert and interested, mouth shut. You follow discussions carefully, but you don't contribute. As a power player, however, you're not simply finding your feet. You're awaiting an opportunity.

When it arrives, you pounce. Sooner or later, one of your fellow directors is going to be guilty of woolly thinking. He's going to voice an opinion that's manifestly absurd. When it happens, you shoot in like a rocket. You take that opinion and coldly analyze it into nothingness. You're utterly ruthless, utterly forceful in your attack. If you like or respect the director in question, you can use your knowledge of *Power Play* to let him down very lightly indeed, to persuade him that, while he is the repository of all knowledge, he has made a mistake this time. If the man is an out and out rival, you can afford to be tougher. But as a power player, you will never attack the man, always the opinion. When you've finished, shut up again for the rest of the meeting.

Your move is so abrupt, so forceful, so unexpected that it will instantly establish your reputation as someone to be reckoned with. You'll find your colleagues tread more warily with you. You'll find your opinion is sought that much more often. You'll find you'll be directly consulted when decisions have to be made. In a conference situation with, for example, representatives of another firm, the technique establishes you instantly as a quiet power man. It also ensures you'll be remembered.

That's an establishment technique. But now you've reached the rarefied realms of top management, the need to establish your level of authority will generally be a lot less pressing than it once was. As a director/shareholder your position with the company has a real measure of security behind it. You can afford to relax a little, to stop pressing on, and start concentrating on avoiding some of the mistakes most often made by men at the top.

One of those mistakes is the failure to delegate.

Power players are particularly prone to this one. They have built up a habit of self-reliance which reaches back to the very start of their working career. They have an enormous reservoir of confidence. They are accustomed to hard work and lots of it. Far too often, this leads them to take on more than they can cope with when they reach the top.

Such an attitude has two major drawbacks. The first is that the power player has no time to enjoy the fruits of his labours. Now he's a success, he's actually working harder than he did on the road to success. A moment's thought should convince him this makes no sense. But he doesn't have time for a moment's thought. He's caught in the success trap. And he's caught because of habit. The second major drawback doesn't affect the successful power player. It affects those under him. As he hogs all the responsible work to himself, they become uneasy and dispirited. Their efficiency suffers, as does their loyalty to the power player. Any power player failing to see the signs will soon find his position undermined, not by his own inefficiency, but by the inefficiency of his department.

The Secret of Successful Delegation

The answer is delegation. And the secret of successful delegation is a curious combination of total trust and total ruthlessness. Give a man a job to do, then forget it. Guide him if he asks for guidance, but don't interfere gratuitously. Don't ask for progress reports. Accept that he's working to the best of his ability and that a series of memos will only waste your time and his. When he completes the job, evaluate the results. If he's done well, tell him so. If possible, tell him so in front of his colleagues. If he's done an acceptable, but not particularly brilliant job, sympathize with him on the difficulties and encourage him to do better next time. If his work is a disaster, fire him.

The ruthless rule applies unless you are fully satisfied there's an excellent reason for the disaster, outside his control. Excuses aren't enough and soft-heartedness shouldn't enter into it. A lengthy past record of good work should obviously be taken into consideration, but the guiding principle is that a man is paid to fulfil a specific function, and if he fails to do so he is simply not earning his money.

Should this situation arise, it's as well to know the *Power Play* technique of dismissal. Use it, if necessary, even on your closest friend. Your 'script' for a *Power Play* dismissal runs, in its entirety, as follows:

'I'm terribly sorry about this, John, but you're fired.'

No preliminaries beforehand. No discussion afterwards, except insofar as it concerns technical details of his term of notice, pension fund contributions and so on. A power player should be able to fire someone in less than two minutes. If it drags beyond that, something's badly wrong.

At first sight this approach seems unnecessarily heartless, even brutal. It's neither. Consider the alternative. You call John into your office, invite him to sit down. You start to talk about the standard of his work. You listen to his excuses. You explain your position. The interview drags on and on. It's painful for you and it's twice as painful for John, who knows perfectly well he's in for the chop and suffers like a fish on a hook through every single minute. And in the end the crunch has to come. Sooner or later you're going to tell him he's fired. So you've saved him nothing and you've subjected him to prolonged suffering. Far better to do the job fast, like pulling a tooth. He'll never thank you for it, but you'll have the consolation of saving his considerable discomfort whether he thanks you for it or not.

Many top executives use their 'fire power' to guard their rear. Every time an up-and-comer looks like threatening their position, they find some excuse to dismiss him. This is a ludicrous error (it strips a company bare of its best young men) and one which, fortunately, power players tend to avoid. Their level of self-confidence is too high for them to feel threatened by young blood. Power players guard their rear by establishing real lines of communication with the young Turks. By building a bond of loyalty. By ensuring the young man gets the recognition he deserves.

In fiction, men frequently reach the top by toppling men already there. In life, this seldom happens. When a man reaches the top, he joins the club. He enlarges the upper strata. Within the upper strata he soon finds his overt guidelines are the rules of business. But if he has studied *Power Play,* he will recognize that, behind it all, the rules of human psychology still apply.

It was those rules the power player studied to reach the top. It is those rules he uses to stay there.

Index